Integrative Systemic Therapy for Families with Children and Adolescents

This book provides an in-depth introduction to the theory and application of Integrative Systemic Therapy (IST) when working with children and their families, allowing clinicians to enhance their skill set and capacity to work effectively with this population.

Written by internationally recognized experts in the field of systemic family therapy, this book describes the development and theoretical underpinnings of IST and essential considerations for working specifically with children and adolescents to develop a strong therapeutic alliance. Readers follow a clinical case involving a multiproblem family through the authors' framework for treatment. Chapters explore how to locate and identify problems, reduce the impact of children-specific problems, and work with constraints pulling from the therapist's arsenal of multisystemic tools. Special attention is given to clinical case formulations and strategies for addressing situations when therapy progress is limited and relational difficulties compound the presenting problems.

This book is suitable for a wide range of mental health professionals as well as students of clinical psychology, counselling, and clinical social work who work regularly or intermittently with children, adolescents, and their families.

Kristoffer J. Whittaker, PhD, is a clinical psychologist practicing at the family counseling office, Senior Researcher at the Modum Bad Psychiatric Center, and Lecturer in the Department of Psychology at the University of Oslo, Norway.

Lennart Lorås, D.Sys.Psych, MA, is Professor at Western Norway University of Applied Sciences and Professor II at VID Specialized University, Norway. He is an internationally recognized leader in the field of Integrative Systemic Therapy (IST), with many years of research and clinical experience in child and adolescent mental health.

The Family Institute Series: Clinical Applications of the Integrative Systemic Therapy (IST) Model

Series editors: Anthony L. Chambers, Douglas C. Breunlin, William P. Russell, and Jay Lawrence Lebow

The Family Institute Series: Clinical Applications of the Integrative Systemic Therapy (IST) Model focuses on elaborating the theory and practice of Integrative Systemic Therapy (IST) and its application to various populations and contexts. Embracing empiricism, diversity, and creativity, the series distills the complex landscape of psychotherapy into clinician friendly guidelines and strategies useful to all practitioners and students in psychology, marriage and family therapy, counseling and the other mental health professions.

Titles in the series:

Integrative Systemic Therapy in Practice
A Clinician's Handbook
William P. Russell, Douglas C. Breunlin, and Bahareh Sahebi

Integrative Systemic Supervision
Training Therapists to Work with Individuals, Couples, and Families
Yaliu He, Nathan Hardy, Adam Fisher, and Neil Venketramen

Integrative Systemic Therapy for Families with Children and Adolescents
A Clinician's Handbook
Kristoffer J. Whittaker and Lennart Lorås

"Whittaker and Lorås' book is a pathbreaking extension of Integrative Systemic Therapy into the domain of child and adolescent problems. This domain has been touched upon in previous IST writings from a high-altitude perspective. Whittaker and Lorås bring that perspective down to 50 feet, where the reader can see and feel the pain and joy of these children and their families as they struggle to address and resolve their problems. In this incredibly thoughtful and practical book, the authors offer systemically oriented therapists a detailed map of the child and adolescent terrain, with specific guidelines and deep wisdom for helping these children and their families."

William Pinsof, *PhD, LMFT, ABBP, Pinsof Family Systems*

"This book is a gem. Whittaker and Lorås show how IST distills insights from many schools of family therapy and relevant research into principles that are exceptionally practical in guiding clinical work with complex, child-focused family problems. This is a cutting-edge guide on how to practice contemporary family therapy. A book that must be read by both therapists in training and experienced clinicians."

Alan Carr, *PhD, Professor of Clinical Psychology, University College Dublin*

"This book is an essential read for clinicians working with families. Accessible IST tools lay the groundwork for theoretical integration, and rich vignettes bring theory to life. It shifts the focus from individual symptoms to layered family dynamics shaped by cultural contexts. It helps therapists navigate the nuances of clinical decision-making."

Yaliu He, *PhD, LMFT, Associate Professor, Iona University, Marriage and Family Therapy Department*

"The book emphasizes the research foundation of the coherent IST model and presents it as a source of reassurance for a resilient future within a systemic perspective on psychotherapy. Here you are introduced to the relational and dialogical core of the model in systemic work, while ensuring that practice remains transparent, reflexive, and responsive to diversity. Working alliances with all family members are highlighted as key tasks, especially with children and young people. The book is highly recommended reading."

Johan Sundelin, *DMSc, Certified Psychologist, Certified Psychotherapist*

Integrative Systemic Therapy for Families with Children and Adolescents

A Clinician's Handbook

Kristoffer J. Whittaker and Lennart Lorås

Routledge
Taylor & Francis Group
NEW YORK AND LONDON

Designed cover image: Getty Images

First published 2027
by Routledge
605 Third Avenue, New York, NY 10158

and by Routledge
4 Park Square, Milton Park, Abingdon, Oxon, OX14 4RN

Routledge is an imprint of the Taylor & Francis Group, an informa business

ISBN: 978-1-041-08430-3 (hbk)
ISBN: 978-1-041-08429-7 (pbk)
ISBN: 978-1-003-64533-7 (ebk)

DOI: 10.4324/9781003645337

Typeset in Sabon
by Apex CoVantage, LLC

Contents

Acknowledgments

We would like to thank our colleagues and collaborators who have contributed to the ongoing development of Integrative Systemic Therapy (IST). We offer special thanks to Bill Russell, Doug Breunlin, and Bill Pinsof. We are also grateful to the many clinicians and families whose experiences continue to inspire us and inform and refine our understanding of systemic practice.

Preface

This volume forms part of *The Family Institute Series: Clinical Applications of the Integrative Systemic Therapy (IST) Model* and focuses on the application of IST with children, adolescents, and their families. The series aims to demonstrate how the conceptual foundations of IST can guide clinical practice across a range of contexts and presenting problems. Earlier volumes have outlined and expanded the general framework of IST and demonstrated its application in clinical practice, including supervision. The present volume focuses on the particular opportunities and challenges that arise when working with children and adolescents within their family systems.

Children and adolescents rarely seek therapy on their own initiative. Instead, they are typically referred by other professionals or brought to therapy by parents or caregivers. The reasons families seek therapy may take many forms. Some are typically framed as individual problems, such as anxiety, depression, or problematic behavior. Others are more often viewed as relational concerns, including school refusal, sibling rivalry, parent–child conflict, or broader family tensions. Regardless of how the problem is initially understood, IST views presenting problems as unfolding within relational contexts. Human difficulties are therefore conceptualized as patterns of interaction that develop and are maintained within families and the wider systems in which they live. From this perspective, therapeutic work with young people necessarily involves engaging with the whole family system.

The aim of this volume is to translate the principles of IST into practical guidance for therapists working with children and adolescents. Throughout the chapters, we illustrate how IST can guide therapists across the phases of therapy, from the first contact with a family, through case formulation and intervention planning, to evaluating progress and concluding treatment. The focus is not only on what therapists do but also on how they conceptualize the therapeutic process. In this way, the book seeks to bridge theory and practice by demonstrating how systemic concepts can inform moment-to-moment clinical decision-making. In doing so, the volume contributes to ongoing efforts within systemic therapy to develop frameworks that integrate conceptual clarity with practical applicability.

This book is written primarily for clinicians working with children, adolescents, and families. It may be particularly useful for marriage and family therapists, psychologists, psychiatrists, social workers, and other professionals who wish to integrate systemic thinking into their clinical practice. At the same time, it is intended to be accessible to students and trainees who are learning to work with families for the first time. Our goal has been to present the concepts of IST in a way that is both theoretically grounded and practically useful.

This volume is organized in two parts. Part I introduces the theoretical and conceptual foundations of IST for work with children, adolescents, and families. To make the material as accessible and practice-oriented as possible, the chapters make extensive use of fictional clinical cases. Chapter 1 provides an overview of IST and its relevance for therapy with young people and their families. Chapter 2 outlines the foundations of family systems theory that underpin the model. Chapter 3 introduces the core conceptual tools of IST, including the blueprint for therapy, the essence diagram, the web of human experience, and constraint theory. Chapter 4 focuses on alliance formation and therapeutic conversations with children, adolescents, and their families. Chapters 5 and 6 introduce the hypothesizing and planning metaframeworks and demonstrate how these structures guide treatment planning.

Part II focuses on clinical practice and follows the therapeutic process step by step. Chapter 7 examines how therapists establish first contact with families and collaboratively define the problem. Chapter 8 demonstrates how systemic case formulations can be developed using the web of human experience. Chapter 9 explores how complex concerns can be reformulated into identifiable problem sequences, while Chapter 10 shows how therapists help families develop and implement solution sequences. Chapter 11 addresses how constraints that limit change can be identified and addressed in therapy. Chapter 12 examines how systematic feedback can be integrated into systemic therapy with children and adolescents. Chapter 13 focuses on evaluating therapeutic progress and conducting endings that consolidate change and strengthen the family's capacity for continued adaptation. Chapter 14 reflects on the implications of the IST framework for therapy with children, adolescents, and their families and concludes the volume. It is our hope that the concepts and practices presented in this volume will assist therapists in supporting families as they navigate the ongoing processes of change and adaptation.

Part I

Chapter 1

Introduction

The first book on Integrative Systemic Therapy (IST) was published in 2018 (Pinsof et al., 2018). It was followed by Routledge's *The Family Institute Series: Clinical Applications of the Integrative Systemic Therapy (IST) Model*, of which the present volume is a part. Previously published volumes in the series include *Integrative Systemic Therapy in Practice* (Russell et al., 2022) and *Integrative Systemic Supervision* (He et al., 2025). Together, these contributions reflect the ongoing development of IST as a comprehensive and evolving framework for clinical practice.

Therapists work in a landscape where human problems are rarely isolated or straightforward. Thus, families arrive in therapy with a mixture of emotional struggles, relational conflicts, developmental challenges, and practical stressors. A parent may be worried about a child's anxiety. Still, at the same time, the couple is experiencing marital tension, financial difficulties are present, and grandparents could hold strong opinions about how the family should function. Similarly, children and adolescents, who are referred to treatment for individual difficulties, need to be met by a therapist who understands how their described difficulties are maintained, not only within their own inner world but also in their closest relationships and broader community. In such situations, linear explanations and interventions focusing on the individual often fall short. What is needed is an approach that can address complexity without losing clarity, one that brings together individual, relational, and contextual perspectives in a coherent therapeutic process. Such an approach is especially important when working with children and adolescents who suffer from both mental and relational distress. Often it is necessary to engage not only their nearest family in an effort to help them improve and recover but also their social networks including extended family, kindergarten, school, and primary healthcare.

IST was developed as a direct response to these challenges. Rather than aligning itself exclusively with one school of thought or one specific method, IST is grounded in the recognition that human problems are multidimensional, and that effective therapy must be both integrative and systemic

DOI: 10.4324/9781003645337-2

(Whittaker & Lorås, 2025). Integrative, because it draws on a wide range of psychological theories and evidence-based practices. Systemic, because it situates problems within interactional sequences and broader contexts rather than reducing them to traits within individuals (Pinsof et al., 2018). This dual orientation enables IST to respond flexibly to the realities of clinical practice, where no client system is identical and where therapists must constantly adapt their strategies to the unique configuration of problems, resources, and goals that each family or individual presents.

At its core, IST aims to create meaningful and sustainable change by enhancing the overall functionality of client systems. It is a client system-centered and problem-solving approach, emphasizing collaboration and the co-construction of strategies that address problem sequences rather than isolated symptoms. Its aim is not only to reduce distress but also to strengthen resilience, communication, and the use of relational and contextual resources (Russell et al., 2022). In practice, IST is applied across diverse contexts: with individuals struggling with anxiety or depression, with couples facing conflict or disconnection, with families adapting to developmental or situational crises, and even within organizational or community systems where systemic tensions affect well-being (Whittaker & Lorås, 2023). By maintaining a flexible, integrative stance, IST equips therapists to work effectively with the complexity of real-world problems while keeping the focus on solutions that matter for clients' lives.

The development of Integrative Systemic Therapy (IST)

For decades, psychotherapy has been characterized by a proliferation of therapeutic approaches, each with its own language, assumptions, and preferred techniques. Approaches such as cognitive behavioral therapy, psychodynamic therapy, solution-focused therapy, and humanistic approaches have all provided valuable insights. Yet practitioners have often found themselves asking: Which approach should I choose, and how can I know whether it will fit the complexity of the clients in front of me?

In an era of increasing specialization and fragmentation, there has been growing recognition that clients often present with overlapping diagnoses, multiple stressors, and diverse cultural backgrounds. Integrative Systemic Therapy (IST) responds to this reality by emphasizing that no single theory holds all the answers (Russell & Breunlin, 2019). Standardized protocols may be effective in research trials with homogeneous populations, but therapists in everyday practice require an approach that can flexibly respond to the heterogeneity of real clients. IST provides such a framework by combining scientific rigor with clinical adaptability, ensuring that therapy is both evidence-based and tailored to the unique needs of each client system (Whittaker & Lorås, 2025). At the same time, IST was developed to bridge the enduring gap between research and practice. By structuring therapy around transparent processes and overarching metaframeworks, it creates a language that is both clinically useful and scientifically testable. This way of structuring the therapeutic process, without oversimplifying its complexity, yields insights that can guide practitioners (Lorås & Whittaker, 2026). In this way, IST stands as both a practice model and a research framework, designed to evolve continuously through the interplay of empirical findings, theoretical advances, and clinical wisdom (Whittaker et al., 2023).

Core orientation: client system-centered and problem-solving

At the heart of Integrative Systemic Therapy (IST) lies a commitment to viewing clients not as isolated individuals but as participants in interconnected relational systems (Russell & Breunlin, 2019). Thus, IST directs attention to the patterns of thought, emotion, and behavior that circulate between family members and shape sequences of distress or resilience. What matters is not only *who* is struggling but *how* difficulties are sustained in the ongoing exchanges of the family system.

This perspective becomes clearer when applied to everyday clinical situations. Consider the case of a child who refuses to attend school. From an individual lens, the problem may be defined as an anxiety disorder within the child, and treatment might focus primarily on coping skills or exposure exercises. Through a systemic lens, however, the child's anxiety is understood in relation to parental pressure, rising conflict between caregivers, and even cultural expectations about academic achievement and responsibility. This shift makes it possible to address both the child's emotional distress and the family's patterns of regulation, thereby widening the scope for meaningful and sustainable change. Another example comes from parent–child conflict. Traditional approaches might label the adolescent as "oppositional" or "defiant" and the parent as "overly controlling" or "inconsistent." IST reframes this interaction as an escalating control-resistance sequence, where each person's reaction is both a response to and a trigger for the other's behavior. The young person's withdrawal or protest may reflect attempts to regain autonomy, while the parent's increased monitoring or insistence may reflect growing anxiety and concern. The problem-solving task is not to "correct" the adolescent or "train" the parent, but to support both in experimenting with new forms of communication and boundaries that reduce escalation and foster mutual understanding and safety. High levels of marital conflict, particularly when unresolved, may have a significant negative impact on children's well-being and development and may also limit their capacity to recover from individual distress (Harold & Sellers, 2018). From an IST perspective, helping parents reformulate and modify problematic relational sequences into more adaptive patterns of interaction may therefore be of substantial benefit. Such changes may not only strengthen the couple relationship but also enhance parental capacity, thereby increasing parents' ability to support their children's emotional and developmental functioning.

The problem-solving focus in IST does not imply simplistic fixes. On the contrary, systemic difficulties are complex and often embedded in multiple layers of the human experience, including biological, psychological, cultural, and relational aspects (Pinsof et al., 2018). Effective solutions emerge through an iterative process of generating hypotheses, co-creating strategies with the family, testing outcomes, and using feedback to refine both understanding and intervention.

Importantly, IST also has an ethical dimension. By framing difficulties as relational sequences rather than individual flaws, it reduces shame and blame. Parents of a struggling child may shift from feeling they have "failed" to recognizing that change can emerge through collective effort. Partners in conflict may move from blaming each other to jointly exploring how their patterns can be reshaped. In this way, IST not only generates solutions but also fosters resilience, compassion, and shared responsibility for change (Whittaker & Tilden, 2022).

Common factors in systemic practice

The common factors are a central element of Integrative Systemic Therapy (IST), emphasizing that therapeutic change is not driven solely by specific models or techniques but also by relational and contextual elements that cut across all effective therapies (Whittaker & Lorås, 2025). Research over the past few decades has consistently shown that therapeutic alliance, empathy, client engagement, and hope are among the strongest predictors of outcome, often more so than the technical orientation of the therapist (Wampold & Imel, 2015). IST incorporates this knowledge systematically. Rather than seeing common factors as background conditions, IST places them at the center of the change process and integrates them intentionally with systemic assessment and intervention. The alliance is cultivated not just between therapist and client but also across subsystems of the family, helping members to reconnect and collaborate on shared goals (Pinsof et al., 2018).

For instance, when a family comes to therapy reporting repeated conflicts around household responsibilities, an integrative systemic therapist does more than analyze the problem sequence. The therapist also works deliberately to strengthen the alliance by acknowledging each person's perspective without judgment. This attention to each family member in fostering the alliance is especially important when working with children and adolescents, who often do not enter therapy with the same agency, motivation, or decision-making authority as their adult family members (Whittaker & Tilden, 2025). By highlighting moments when the family has successfully cooperated in the past, the therapist instills hope that new solutions are possible. Collaboration is fostered by inviting each member to help define what a "better pattern" would look like, ensuring that change is co-owned rather than imposed. In this way, the therapeutic process integrates common factors into IST, demonstrating how empathy, alliance, and hope become active ingredients in restructuring problem sequences.

Combining specific models systematically

Many therapeutic approaches that attempt to select techniques from a wide range of psychotherapy traditions without a clear rationale or underlying principles risk becoming eclectic (Whittaker & Tilden, 2022). Integrative Systemic Therapy (IST) avoids this by offering a structured framework that guides the selection of models, when to use them, and how to integrate them into the systemic formulation (Pinsof et al., 2018; Russell et al., 2023).

At the core of this framework is the recognition that no single theory can adequately address the full complexity of human difficulties. Families present with problems that simultaneously involve biological vulnerability, relational strain, developmental challenges, and sociocultural pressures. By drawing on multiple models, IST allows the therapist to flexibly respond to these layers while maintaining a coherent systemic perspective (Whittaker & Tilden, 2022; Whittaker & Lorås, 2025).

For example, consider a child presenting depressive symptoms. A purely cognitive behavioral approach might focus on the child's negative thoughts and avoidance behaviors. While such strategies can be helpful, they risk overlooking how parental conflict or cultural expectations contribute to the child's despair. In IST, the therapist might integrate cognitive behavioral techniques to support the child's coping, attachment-based interventions to strengthen parental responsiveness, and systemic enactments to shift family interactional patterns. The combination is not random; it is guided by the evolving systemic hypotheses and the blueprint for therapy, which link interventions to identified problem sequences (Pinsof et al., 2018). By acknowledging that each model has strengths and limitations, IST positions the therapist not as the possessor of a single truth but as a collaborator who draws on diverse knowledge bases in the service of the family's goals (Lebow, 2019). In this way, integration becomes not eclecticism, but a disciplined practice of tailoring therapy to the evolving relational patterns that sustain a problem (Whittaker & Tilden, 2022; Whittaker & Lorås, 2025; Russell et al., 2023).

The benefit of combining models systematically is twofold. First, it enhances the therapist's flexibility, allowing interventions to be tailored to the family's unique needs and contexts (He et al., 2023). Second, it preserves coherence: the therapist avoids fragmentation by continuously anchoring interventions in the systemic formulation. Combining models systematically protects both therapist and family from the confusion that arises when methods are applied without a guiding logic (Whittaker & Tilden, 2022).

Concluding remarks

In sum, Integrative Systemic Therapy (IST) emerged to meet the growing demand for therapeutic approaches that could hold complexity without collapsing into reductionism. By integrating multiple theories, highlighting common factors, and situating all problems within systemic interaction, IST offers both a practical method and a flexible framework for therapists. Its client-system orientation ensures that therapy is not about fixing individuals in isolation but about fostering healthier, more adaptive patterns within the systems where people live and develop.

As we bring this chapter to a close, it may be helpful to briefly recall the main threads of IST: its historical development, its orientation as client system-centered and problem-solving, its recognition of common therapeutic factors, and its systematic integration of diverse models. The chapters that follow build on these foundations by showing how IST can be applied across a wide range of clinical contexts to help children and adolescents and their families.

Through a combination of theory and case illustrations, readers are invited not only to understand IST in principle but also to experience how systemic and integrative practice can open new possibilities, strengthen relationships, and support meaningful changes in the lives of clients. Because this volume focuses on working with children, adolescents, and their families, Chapter 2 is dedicated to family systems theory and how it informs integrative systemic practice.

Building on this theoretical foundation, the main body of the book draws on fictional clinical examples to illustrate how IST concepts and competencies, including alliance formation, hypothesis formulation, and problem-solving, are implemented in practice. Each chapter concludes with a self-reflection task designed to help readers consolidate and integrate the material.

References

Harold, G. T., & Sellers, R. (2018). Annual Research Review: Interparental conflict and youth psychopathology: An evidence review and practice focused update.

Journal of Child Psychology and Psychiatry, *59*(4), 374–402. https://doi.org/10.1111/jcpp.12893
He, Y., Hardy, N., Fisher, A., & Venketramen, N. (2025). *Integrative systemic supervision: Training therapists to work with individuals, couples, and families*. Taylor & Francis.
He, Y., Hardy, N. R., Fisher, A. R., & Lokotama, I. (2023). Development of the integrative systemic therapist. *Fokus på Familien* [Focus on the family], *4*(51), 315–331. https://doi.org/10.18261/fokus.51.4.4
Lebow, J. (2019). Current issues in the practice of integrative couple and family therapy. *Family Process*, *58*(3), 610–628. https://doi.org/10.1111/famp.12473
Lorås, L., & Whittaker, K. J. (2026). Integrative systemic therapy. In O. Smoliak, E. Tseliou, T. Strong, S. Bava, & P. Muntigl (Eds.), *The Routledge international handbook of postmodern therapies* (pp. 249–262). Routledge.
Pinsof, W. M., Breunlin, D. C., Russell, W. P., Lebow, J. L., Rampage, C., & Chambers, A. L. (2018). *Integrative systemic therapy: Metaframeworks for problem solving with individuals, couples, and families*. American Psychological Association. https://doi.org/10.1037/0000055-000
Russell, W. P., & Breunlin, D. C. (2019). Transcending therapy models and managing complexity: Suggestions from integrative systemic therapy. *Family Process*, *3*(58), 641–655. https://doi.org/10.1111/famp.12482
Russell, W. P., Breunlin, D. C., & Lofton, H. C. (2023). Integrative systemic therapy: A feedback-driven perspective. *Fokus på Familien* [Focus on the family], *4*(50), 293–314. https://doi.org/10.18261/fokus.51.4.3
Russell, W. P., Breunlin, D. C., & Sahebi, B. (2022). *Integrative systemic therapy in practice: A clinician's handbook*. Routledge.
Wampold, B. E., & Imel, Z. E. (2015). *The great psychotherapy debate: The evidence for what makes psychotherapy work*. Routledge. https://doi.org/10.4324/9780203582015
Whittaker, K. J., & Lorås, L. (2023). Integrativ Systemisk Terapi som tilnærming i arbeid med sammensatte problemer [Integrative Systemic Therapy as a therapeutic approach to compounded problems]. *Fokus på familien* [Focus on the family], *4*(51), 332–348. https://doi.org/10.18261/fokus.51.4.5
Whittaker, K. J., & Lorås, L. (2025). Integrativ systemisk terapi [Integrative systemic therapy]. In L. Lorås & O. Ness (Eds.), *Håndbok i familieterapi* [Handbook in family therapy] (pp. 283–298). Fagbokforlaget.
Whittaker, K. J., & Tilden, T. (2022). Integrativ systemisk terapi: Metateori og psykoterapeutisk praksis. *Fokus På Familien* [Focus on the family], *50*(3), 190–206. https://doi.org/10.18261/fokus.50.3.2
Whittaker, K. J., & Tilden, T. (2025). Fellesfaktorer i par og familieterapi [Common factors in couple and family therapy]. In L. Lorås & O. Ness (Eds.), *Håndbok i familieterapi* [Handbook in family therapy] (pp. 83–97). Fagbokforlaget.
Whittaker, K., Stokkebekk, J., Lorås, L., & Tilden, T. (2023). Researching what we practice—The paradigm of systemic family research: Part 2. *Family Process*, *62*(3), 961–975. https://doi.org/10.1111/famp.12921

Chapter 2

Family Systems Theory

Introduction

Integrative Systemic Therapy (IST) is a metatheoretical perspective grounded in family systems theory (He et al., 2023). This anchoring ensures that therapy is not confined to the individual but addresses the complex interplay of subsystems in which children and families are embedded. A solid understanding of family systems theory is therefore essential for grasping how change unfolds when systemic interventions are applied to address problems within a client system. It provides the conceptual foundation for understanding patterns of interaction, mutual influence, and the processes through which therapeutic change emerges in work with children, adolescents, and their families. In IST, these foundational ideas are further developed through the hypothesizing metaframeworks and the web of human experience. Together, they organize knowledge about problems, constraints, and resources into clinically useful competencies, as elaborated in Chapter 5.

Family systems theory conceptualizes families as dynamic and self-regulating systems in which individual, relational, and contextual factors are interwoven and continuously influence one another (Priest, 2025). From this perspective, core elements such as autonomy, adaptation, attachment, triangulation, and sociocultural context provide a comprehensive framework for understanding family stability and change over time (Priest & Lorås, 2026). For family systems theory to be meaningful within IST as a clinical and academic framework, it must first be situated within a shared understanding of what a theory is and why theoretical frameworks are essential for practice and scholarship. Because the concept of a system is central to this theoretical foundation, the chapter will then clarify what is meant by a system before turning to its specific application in families. Finally, the discussion will demonstrate how family systems theory can be applied within IST to analyze and address challenging life situations by identifying patterns that either foster or hinder a family's ability to adapt, regulate emotions, and maintain relational balance.

DOI: 10.4324/9781003645337-3

To ground the theoretical discussion, the Johansen family will be used as a case example throughout this chapter. Living in Arkansas, Anna and Erik are raising their three children, Emma (14), Jonas (10), and Sofia (6), while navigating Erik's recent job loss, Anna's demanding work schedule, and the children's different developmental needs.

What is a theory?

For family systems theory to serve as a meaningful foundation within Integrative Systemic Therapy (IST), it is necessary to clarify what we mean by a theory. IST is presented as a comprehensive and evolving framework for working with children, adolescents, and their families. A shared understanding of theory is therefore essential. Priest (2021, p. 4) defines a theory as a systematic network of concepts, definitions, and hypotheses aimed at explaining, understanding, and predicting real-world phenomena. Theories thus move beyond description. They offer explanatory models that illuminate underlying mechanisms and processes of change.

Within IST, theory functions like a map that helps therapists navigate complex relational landscapes (Priest & Lorås, 2026). It supports an understanding of how emotions, roles, communication patterns, power dynamics, and cultural contexts intersect in family life. In therapeutic work with children and adolescents, this perspective is particularly important. Family systems theory encourages us to understand children's symptoms not as isolated intrapsychic problems, but as meaningful expressions of interactional processes within the family system (Priest, 2025). This framing supports integrative systemic interventions that address both the young person's distress and the relational dynamics that sustain it.

For theory to remain clinically relevant within IST, it must be grounded in a clear understanding of the phenomena it seeks to explain. Because family systems theory conceptualizes families as relational systems, the next step is to clarify what is meant by a system and why a systemic perspective is essential in therapeutic work with children, adolescents, and their families.

What is a system?

von Bertalanffy (1969) defined a system as "a set of elements in mutual relationship." Mutuality means that the elements influence one another in ways that produce qualities that cannot be reduced to the individual parts. For a group of elements to constitute a system, the internal relations must be qualitatively different from interactions with the external environment. It is these internal connections that give the system its identity and boundaries.

Donella Meadows (2008) expanded and specified this understanding by defining a system as "an interconnected set of elements that is coherently organized to achieve something" (p. 11). According to Meadows, a system consists of three main components: (1) the elements, (2) the interconnections between elements, and (3) a function or purpose. Elements may be physical, such as organs in a body, or social, such as members of a family. The interconnections describe how elements influence one another, for instance, through communication, emotional responses, or role distribution. The purpose refers to what the system seeks to maintain or achieve, sometimes explicitly stated, as in a sports team seeking to win a championship, and other times implicitly understood, as in a family striving to provide emotional safety for its children.

Crucially, Meadows emphasized that a system is not defined primarily by its elements, but by the interconnections and shared purpose that hold it together. A football team and a jazz band may both consist of the same number of individuals, yet their purposes and interaction patterns generate very different systemic qualities. Many systems are adaptive and self-organizing, meaning they adjust their organization and patterns to fulfil their purpose more effectively. This is particularly evident in social systems such as families, where roles and interactions shift in response to stressors, developmental transitions, and the changing needs of children and adolescents.

Wong and colleagues (2023) elaborated this view by describing systems as dynamic combinations of elements and relations in which specific organizational patterns are reinforced while others are discarded, depending on how well they support the system's purpose. Structures and interaction patterns are therefore understood as products of a developmental process that is continuously adjusted over time. In families, such processes are central to Integrative Systemic Therapy (IST) as a comprehensive and evolving framework for working with children, adolescents, and their families. For example, a family in which one child repeatedly takes on the role of mediator in parental conflicts illustrates how new interactional patterns may emerge to restore balance and reduce tension. Although such a role may be burdensome for the child, it may persist because it serves the larger systemic purpose of maintaining stability. Similarly, when a child develops anxiety, avoidance behaviors may initially reduce stress for both the child and the parents, but over time reinforce the problem. Meadows (2008) described such dynamics as feedback loops, which can either stabilize or amplify processes within the system.

From this perspective, a family can be understood as a group of people in enduring, reciprocal relationships whose internal interactions are qualitatively different from interactions with outsiders. Families develop patterns and structures to meet shared needs, manage challenges, and ensure continuity over time. These patterns are not random but emerge from earlier experiences that have proved functional for the system's survival and coherence, even if they may at times be restrictive or burdensome for individual members.

Thus, a system may be defined as an organized whole in which interdependent parts interact through recurrent patterns and processes. The relationships between the parts are as significant as the parts themselves. Systems maintain their structure and function through boundaries that distinguish them from their environment, while simultaneously adapting to and being shaped by external conditions. This dynamic interaction allows a system to preserve stability while adjusting to new developmental and contextual challenges.

Family systems theory as a framework for understanding family interactions

Family systems theory provides a framework for understanding how individuals within a family both shape and are shaped by each other's behavior, and how these interactions differ from relationships outside the family (Priest, 2025). The family system comprises several interconnected subsystems: genetic, individual, attachment, and triangulation systems, all embedded within a broader sociocultural context (Priest & Lorås, 2026). Each of these subsystems is both autonomous and adaptive. They maintain themselves through internal processes while also responding to stimuli from internal and external environments. These responses may involve changes that are reversible or irreversible. The autonomy and adaptive capacity of the family system rest on three fundamental processes: (1) responses to threats, (2) the experience of belonging, and (3) the need for individual development. While these processes can be distinguished analytically, they are interconnected, follow recognizable patterns, and together shape the unique dynamics of each family. These processes also form core components of the hypothesizing metaframeworks. In particular, belonging and individuality reflect key organizing dynamics within the organization metaframework (see Chapter 5).

The genetic system encompasses inheritance, evolutionary mechanisms, and epigenetic processes, which form the foundation for the individual system. The individual system includes the body's biological structures, including the nervous system, the cardiovascular system, and the brain. These structures give rise to emotions, cognitions, and identity, which in turn shape how people respond to both interpersonal interactions and physical stimuli, such as heat or cold. When two people establish a close relationship, such as the parent–child dyad, an attachment system emerges. This system involves not only observable interactions but also internal biological and psychological processes. Because individuals are typically engaged in multiple attachment bonds simultaneously, relationships are rarely experienced in isolation. It is at the intersection of these overlapping attachments that triangulation can arise, as third parties become involved in dyadic tensions in ways that may either stabilize or destabilize the family system.

These systemic dynamics can be illustrated through the Johansen family, who are navigating several stressors such as Erik's recent job loss, Anna's demanding work schedule, and the children's differing developmental needs. The situation highlights the continuous interaction between family subsystems. Erik's unemployment challenges the couple's attachment system, Anna's work stress influences the children's sense of belonging, and the siblings' different ages and needs create ongoing negotiations of individuality. At the same time, cultural expectations about gender roles and professional identity shape how Anna and Erik experience themselves and each other as parents and partners. The Johansen family thus exemplifies how family systems adapt to both internal pressures and external sociocultural influences, and how these adaptations affect each member differently while still being part of a shared systemic process.

The triangulation system, for example, becomes visible when 10-year-old Jonas steps into the role of mediator during conflicts between his parents. Instead of addressing each other directly, Anna may turn to Jonas with her frustrations, while he attempts to reassure her or soften Erik's responses. Although this temporarily reduces open conflict, it risks placing Jonas in a caretaking role that distracts him from his own developmental needs. Such dynamics illustrate how children can become entangled in their parents' struggles, and how systemic balance is sought through patterns that may carry hidden long-term costs.

The sociocultural system and its significance for the family

The family system is also shaped by the sociocultural system in which it is embedded. This system encompasses the broader social, cultural, and environmental conditions that influence how families function. It encompasses values, norms, economic and political conditions, and cultural narratives that shape daily family life, allocate roles, and inform how families respond to challenges (Priest & Lorås, 2026). Values and attitudes are transmitted across generations through social learning, shaping family identity and internal relational patterns.

Cultural norms play a central role in this process. They shape what is considered acceptable parenting, how responsibilities are divided between mothers and fathers, and how partnership and caregiving are practiced (Priest, 2025). Families are also influenced by their connections to wider social arenas, including schools, workplaces, friendship networks, and local communities. These external relationships can provide vital support but may also create stress, depending on how they are integrated into family life. Economic and political conditions are equally significant, since access to education and health services, financial security, and the impact of public policies all directly affect how families negotiate their daily lives. For example, a parenting style shaped by ideals of independence and individual achievement may come into tension with a child's need for emotional closeness, particularly in contexts that highly value self-reliance. Similarly, economic insecurity or marginalization can create stress that undermines the family's ability to manage conflict and maintain stable and supportive relationships. Within family systems theory, the sociocultural system is understood as a dynamic external structure that interacts with internal family processes, sometimes reinforcing and at other times challenging the family's capacity for adaptation and development (Priest & Lorås, 2026).

This reciprocal relationship between family and environment is also reflected in the language used to describe family members. Terms such as "father," "daughter," or "aunt" are not only relational markers but also carriers of cultural assumptions about gender, power, and expectations. Roles also shift over time, as a daughter may later become a mother and a father may become a grandfather, positions that are culturally coded and socially contextualized. In the Johansen family, these dynamics are clearly visible. Erik's unemployment has created financial strain in a community where professional identity is closely tied to self-worth. Anna's extended family places strong emphasis on traditional gender roles, expecting her to prioritize caregiving at home even while she works long hours outside the household. These external pressures also shape their children. Emma negotiates adolescence in a peer culture that values autonomy, Jonas experiences strong expectations of responsibility at school, and Sofia depends heavily on her teacher's support when her mother is absent. These sociocultural pressures not only affect Anna and Erik's negotiations as a couple but also shape the children's sense of security, belonging, and autonomy.

By situating the family within its broader sociocultural context, family systems theory enables an understanding of how internal and external processes interact over time, shaping the family's capacity to adapt, maintain cohesion, and foster development.

Autonomy and adaptation in the family system

For a family system to maintain itself as a distinct and functional entity, it must possess a degree of autonomy. Autonomy here refers to the system's ability to establish and sustain patterns of interaction among its members that distinguish it from the environment and provide it with a clear direction or purpose. For instance, some families may develop consistent routines for managing conflict, such as setting aside weekly meetings to discuss disagreements. This type of internal regeneration enables the family to maintain its own structure, regardless of how it may be perceived in peer groups, the wider community, or the media. Such patterns express the family's autonomous capacity to regulate itself based on its own needs, values, and goals. Autonomy alone, however, is not sufficient. A system must also be adaptive. It needs to register signals from both the environment and its internal processes and respond with changes that may be reversible or irreversible, depending on the intensity and significance of the stimulus.

The Johansen family is a helpful illustration of how autonomy and adaptation work together. Following Erik's job loss, the family experienced financial strain and heightened tension. In response, Anna established new routines that promoted stability, such as scheduling regular family dinners and fostering open conversations with the children about their concerns and worries. At the same time, the family adjusted their spending patterns and redistributed household responsibilities to cope with the new situation. These adaptive responses helped preserve the family's integrity and identity as a cohesive unit, despite the external pressures. This example illustrates how autonomy and adaptation work together to support the family's survival and ongoing development.

Three fundamental processes: threat response, belonging, and individuality

Autonomy and adaptation in the family system are created and sustained through three central processes: (1) threat response, (2) belonging, and (3) individuality (Priest, 2025).

Threat response

Threat response refers to the interactions that are activated when the system or its members are exposed to danger or distress. These may involve physical, emotional, or relational threats. Classic reactions such as fight, flight, or freeze are examples of these processes. Such responses are not necessarily a sign of vulnerability, but rather an expression of the fundamental human need for safety. The activation of threat responses can also lead to structural changes in the family system, shaping both temporary adjustments and longer-term shifts in functioning.

In the Johansen family, Erik's job loss created insecurity that triggered different forms of threat responses. Anna responded with increased activity and control, working long hours and organizing routines in an effort to maintain stability, reflecting a fight-or-flight response. At 10 years old, Jonas often attempted to mediate between his parents to reduce conflict, which can be understood as a strategy to preserve attachment bonds. Sofia, at 6, reacted with clinginess and distress when separated from her mother, reflecting an attachment-seeking response under conditions of perceived threat. These examples demonstrate how threat responses are embedded in systemic patterns, affecting each member differently while still contributing to the family's collective adaptation.

Belonging

Belonging refers to the processes that sustain relationships within the family system. These include expressions of love and emotional support as well as control, loyalty, and shared rules. Belonging is essential for family cohesion but may sometimes create tension when it collides with individual developmental needs.

In the Johansen family, belonging is expressed in both supportive and challenging ways. Erik emphasizes the importance of shared meals and family time as a way of maintaining closeness, particularly during periods of stress. Yet these practices sometimes clash with Emma's growing need for independence at the age of 14. When her parents insist on routines that limit her social activities, she may respond with withdrawal or defiance, illustrating how efforts to preserve belonging can inadvertently create friction with her push for autonomy.

Individuality

Individuality refers to the recognition that each family member is also an independent person with unique needs, emotions, and goals. The balance of the system depends on how well it accommodates both the need for belonging and the need for self-expression. When belonging is emphasized too strongly, individuality may be suppressed, while too little emphasis on shared identity can result in isolation and fragmentation.

In the Johansen family, Emma's adolescence illustrates the tension between belonging and individuality. At 14, she seeks privacy and independence, wanting more time with peers and less parental oversight. Anna and Erik, concerned with maintaining family cohesion during Erik's unemployment and Anna's long work hours, sometimes respond with stricter rules and closer monitoring. Such responses can lead Emma to withdraw or push back firmly, reflecting her struggle to assert individuality within a family system that also places substantial value on belonging.

Belonging and individuality in the family system

In addition to threat response, the processes of belonging and individuality are central mechanisms in the inner dynamics of the family system. These processes interact with threat responses and are crucial for the formation, maintenance, and regulation of relationships over time.

Belonging processes include all forms of interaction that help sustain connections among family members. This involves expressions of love, support, care, and closeness, as well as more controlling or structuring interactions that aim to secure cohesion and stability. For example, family members may influence each other's behavior through norms, rules, or expectations that are designed to preserve unity. This may take the form of strong family rules, social control, or close emotional monitoring, particularly in families experiencing crises or stress. Belonging processes are therefore both confirming relationships and maintaining the system, helping to keep the family system coherent and functional.

Individuality refers to the recognition that each family member is also an autonomous person with their own goals, preferences, and emotions. Family systems theory posits that a balance must be struck between an individual's need for autonomy and the family's need for cohesion (Priest, 2025). When excessive demands for belonging suppress individuality, autonomy is undermined, potentially leading to a loss of personal integrity. Conversely, when emphasis on individuality is at the expense of connection, the sense of family belonging can diminish. A healthy family system, therefore, provides space for individuals to grow and express themselves, while ensuring that they remain integrated into a supportive and meaningful whole (Priest & Lorås, 2026).

The dynamic interplay between belonging and individuality is highly vulnerable to imbalance. When belonging processes become too dominant, they can trigger threat responses in one or more members of the system, which in turn intensifies the need to assert individuality. This often occurs when belonging processes are experienced as invasive or controlling. For example, in the Johansen family, Anna and Erik sometimes attempt to closely monitor Emma's activities, from her school performance to her choice of friends. Although these actions reflect their care and concern, Emma often experiences them as limiting her independence. In response, she may withdraw, keep secrets, or cultivate a separate life outside her parents' awareness. This withdrawal tends to increase her parents' anxiety, which can lead them to tighten control even further. Such cycles illustrate a mutually reinforcing dynamic in which both parents and children attempt to protect their needs yet end up making the relationship more fragile and rigid.

The ability of the family system to support both belonging and individuality is thus essential for its functionality and growth. When the system makes space for both cohesion and autonomy, family members are more likely to handle stress constructively. Achieving this balance, however, requires ongoing adaptation and negotiation, especially in the face of changes or crises that challenge established relational patterns.

Application of family systems theory in challenging life situations

The Johansen family exemplifies how family systems theory offers a lens for examining the various layers of family life under stress. Anna and Erik are navigating Erik's unemployment, Anna's demanding work schedule, and the children's diverse developmental needs. Each of these pressures activates systemic processes of belonging, individuality, and threat response, revealing how families function as both autonomous and adaptive systems.

From a systemic perspective, Erik's withdrawal and Anna's pursuit reflect complementary but potentially rigid coping strategies. Their pursue–withdraw pattern may offer short-term stability, but simultaneously displaces unresolved tension into the parenting relationship. Emma, entering adolescence, becomes the focal point of their anxieties, and triangulation emerges when her behavior is used as a substitute arena for marital conflict. This pattern is not random but follows recognizable systemic logics, where unresolved dyadic stress is redistributed into other relational subsystems.

The children's roles highlight the adaptive, yet costly strategies that families use to regulate distress. Emma's search for autonomy aligns with her developmental needs, but it is intensified by her parents' struggle to strike a balance between closeness and independence. Jonas steps into a mediating position, reflecting both loyalty and the burden of premature responsibility. Sofia responds with increased clinginess, expressing vulnerability and a heightened need for security when relational tensions in the family rise. Each child responds differently, yet their actions are interconnected, forming part of the family's collective effort to maintain stability.

The Johansen family also illustrates how internal processes are inextricably linked to external contexts. Cultural expectations about gender roles place additional strain on Anna and Erik's negotiations, with Anna's parents reinforcing traditional caregiving norms and Erik experiencing stigma tied to unemployment. These external pressures amplify internal tensions, demonstrating how the sociocultural system continuously shapes the family's sense of belonging, identity, and adequacy. The interaction between subsystems highlights that resilience is not solely located within individuals but rather emerges or falters in the dynamic exchange between family members and their environment.

Family systems theory further emphasizes that these dynamics unfold across time. The Johansen family's responses to current stressors are layered upon earlier adaptations. Erik's tendency to withdraw has roots in previous relational experiences, while Anna's problem-solving reflects long-standing patterns of taking responsibility. The children's positions of Emma as independent, Jonas as responsible, and Sofia as dependent may offer temporary stability but risk crystallizing into rigid roles if maintained over time. Attending to these temporal trajectories helps practitioners identify not only how families stabilize themselves in the present but also how they may evolve or become constrained in the future.

The Johansen family demonstrates how systemic concepts can guide attention to leverage points rather than provide fixed solutions. The pursue-and-withdraw cycle indicates where marital dialogue might be supported, triangulation shows where parent and child alliances need recalibration, and children's differentiated roles highlight both vulnerabilities and resources within the sibling subsystem. Far from being abstract, these concepts offer therapists a practical framework for understanding how belonging, individuality, and threat responses are negotiated in real time. The case thus illustrates how family systems theory opens possibilities for intervention by mapping both stability and potential transformation within everyday family life.

Concluding remarks

Family systems theory provides a comprehensive framework for understanding families as dynamic and self-regulating systems. Central to this perspective is the continuous negotiation of autonomy, adaptation, belonging, and individuality within a broader sociocultural context. These systemic processes shape both stability and change. They show how stressors such as financial strain, developmental transitions, or shifting cultural expectations reverberate across subsystems and influence attachment bonds, sibling relationships, and parental roles. Family systems theory equips therapists to trace these ripple effects, anticipate emerging patterns, and identify where the balance between belonging and individuality, or safety and growth, becomes strained.

In clinical practice, this theoretical lens enables therapists to move beyond individual symptoms and situate difficulties within the broader context of systemic interactions. Interventions are then designed not only to relieve distress but also to strengthen the family's adaptive capacity. Attending to systemic processes enables therapists to guide families in ways that support flexible responses to stress and restore balance when relationships become polarized. It also helps mobilize relational resources that allow members to experience both security and independence. Family systems theory, therefore, does more than explain family functioning; it provides a foundation for systemic practice that helps therapists navigate complex and emotionally charged situations. By viewing families as interconnected systems capable of resilience and transformation, therapists are invited to see conflict not only as a threat but also as a potential opening for growth. Vulnerability, in turn, can be seen not only as a risk but also as a gateway to recognition and deeper connection.

Looking forward, grounding therapeutic work in family systems theory ensures that Integrative Systemic Therapy (IST) remains equipped to address the evolving challenges faced by families. As societal expectations, cultural norms, and external stressors continue to shift, this step provides practitioners with the tools to support families in navigating these changes while maintaining a sense of stability, fostering a sense of belonging, and creating space for individuality to flourish.

Self-reflections task

1. What patterns do you see in a family that both help them cope and at the same time keep problems going?
2. In your own family or a family you work with, how is the balance between closeness and independence expressed in everyday interactions?
3. What role does a child or adolescent seem to take in the family, and how might this be connected to the challenges the family is facing?

References

He, Y., Hardy, N. R., Fisher, A. R., & Lokotama, I. (2023). Development of the integrative systemic therapist. *Fokus på Familien* [Focus on the family], *4*(51), 315–331. https://doi.org/10.18261/fokus.51.4.4

Meadows, D. (2008). *Thinking in systems: A primer*. Chelsea Green Publishing.

Priest, J. (2021). *The science of family systems theory*. Routledge. https://doi.org/10.4324/9780367854591

Priest, J. (2025). *The science of family systems theory*. Routledge. https://doi.org/10.4324/9781003491972

Priest, J., & Lorås, L. (2026). *Familiesystemteori. Teori, evidens og praksis* [Family systems theory. Theory, evidence and practice]. Fagbokforlaget.

von Bertalanffy, L. (1969). *General system theory: Foundations, development, applications*. George Braziller.

Wong, M. L., Cleland, C. E., Arend Jr., D., Bartlett, S., Cleaves, H. J., Demarest, H., Prabhu, A., Lunine, J. I., & Hazen, R. M. (2023). On the roles of function and selection in evolving systems. *Proceedings of the National Academy of Sciences*, *120*(43), e2310223120. https://doi.org/10.1073/pnas.2310223120

Chapter 3

Core Concepts of IST

Introduction

Integrative Systemic Therapy (IST) is guided by and adapted to the client's needs according to several core concepts. In this chapter, we will present *the IST blueprint*, *the essence diagram*, *the web of human experience*, *constraint theory*, and *the 12 IST guidelines*. Two other key concepts, the *hypothesizing* and *planning metaframeworks*, will also be briefly introduced here, but are discussed in detail in Chapters 5 and 6. These core concepts form the theoretical and practical foundation of IST and will be applied throughout this book. When necessary, the reader is encouraged to revisit the relevant sections. The purpose of this chapter is to provide a concise overview of the central concepts that inform IST; for a more comprehensive and technical treatment of these ideas including an explanation of the IST metatheory (i.e., *the five pillars of IST*), see *Integrative Systemic Therapy: Metaframeworks for Problem Solving With Individuals, Couples, and Families* (Pinsof et al., 2018).

The blueprint for therapy

The blueprint for therapy (see Figure 3.1) is, in many ways, the most fundamental concept in Integrative Systemic Therapy (IST). It describes the therapeutic process as a dynamic and recursive cycle involving four interconnected steps: (H) hypothesizing, (P) planning, (C) conversing, and (F) feedback (Pinsof et al., 2018). Although hypothesizing is presented as Step 1 in the following description of the blueprint, the entry point is context-dependent, and the process is recursive rather than linear. At times, it may begin with the therapist receiving information from the client (i.e., feedback); at other times, therapist and client may begin by engaging in conversation.

DOI: 10.4324/9781003645337-4

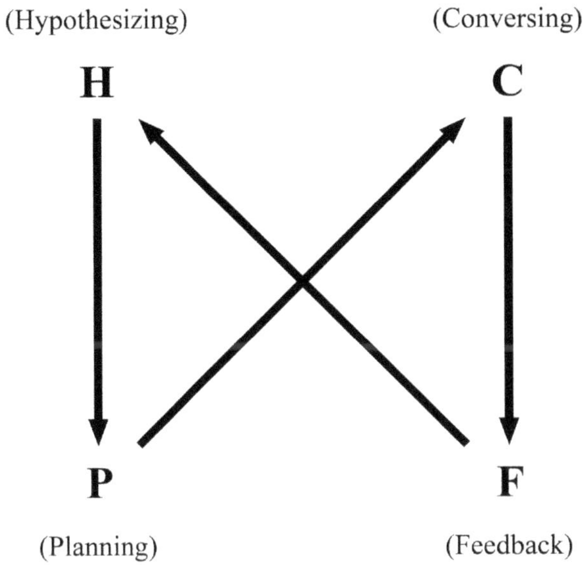

Figure 3.1 The Blueprint for IST

1. *Hypothesizing*, which relates to the *hypothesizing metaframework*, is an active and collaborative process. Here, the therapist uses the client's feedback to make sense of the client system's difficulties, resources, and possible ways forward. These hypotheses are always provisional and are continuously revised as therapy unfolds. Hypotheses are either confirmed, disconfirmed, or adjusted as new feedback emerges.
2. *Planning*, which aligns with the *planning metaframework*, refers to the therapist's clinical decisions based on the current working hypotheses. These decisions can involve broader treatment strategies developed from one session to the next, targeting problem sequences and potential constraints, or to in-the-moment choices such as when to use affective validation, reframing, or enactments.
3. *Conversing* is the task of implementing the selected interventions within the therapeutic dialogue. Through conversing, the therapist co-constructs meaning with clients, facilitates emotional and relational change, and strengthens the therapeutic alliance that sustains the process of change.
4. *Feedback* refers to the ongoing verbal, emotional, behavioral, and relational information that guides therapeutic decision-making. Most feedback emerges naturally in the room, through how family members interact, how they respond to the therapist's interventions, what emotions surface (or do not), and the stories they choose to share. Other forms of feedback are gathered systematically through questionnaires

(see Chapter 12), including self-report and therapist-rated measures, as well as structured clinical interviews. At its core, feedback is what keeps therapy on track. It allows the therapist to refine hypotheses, adjust interventions when needed, and remain attuned to how change is unfolding in real time.

This chapter addresses work with both children and adolescents. While the opening vignette involves a younger child, later sections also include examples from adolescence. In the following, we present a short vignette exemplifying the use of the blueprint in therapy: Following the family's previous session, the therapist holds a working hypothesis (**H**) concerning the interaction of *Heidi*, the mother of *Magnus*, a 5-year-old boy who struggles with frequent outbursts of anger. The therapist hypothesizes that Heidi finds it difficult to understand the emotions underlying her son's anger tantrums. Accordingly, the therapist plans (**P**) to explore this dynamic with both Heidi and Magnus in the next session.

As the session begins (**C**), the therapist speaks:

Therapist: "I've been thinking about our last meeting and was wondering if we could spend some time talking about how you, Heidi, respond when Magnus has his anger tantrums. It seems like it can be hard to understand why there is much anger. Would that be okay?"

Heidi: *(nods in agreement)*

*The therapist observes Heidi's nonverbal communication (***F***). Magnus, who is sitting next to his mother on the couch, quietly playing with a fidget spinner, appears to be listening. The therapist gently turns to him.*

Therapist: *"What do you think, Magnus? Does Mummy know why there is so much anger?"*

Without looking up, Magnus gives a small shake of his head (**F**). Receiving these nonverbal confirmations from both mother and son, the therapist recognizes the relevance of her working hypothesis and continues to explore the theme further.

The essence of IST, web of human experience, and lifting constraints

The essence diagram of problem-solving in IST (see Figure 3.2) represents a sequential guide to the therapeutic process from intake to termination. *The blueprint for therapy* is applied throughout each step of *the essence diagram*, mapping how therapy unfolds as a collaborative and feedback-driven process of identifying and resolving problem sequences and, when necessary, lifting the constraints that maintain them.

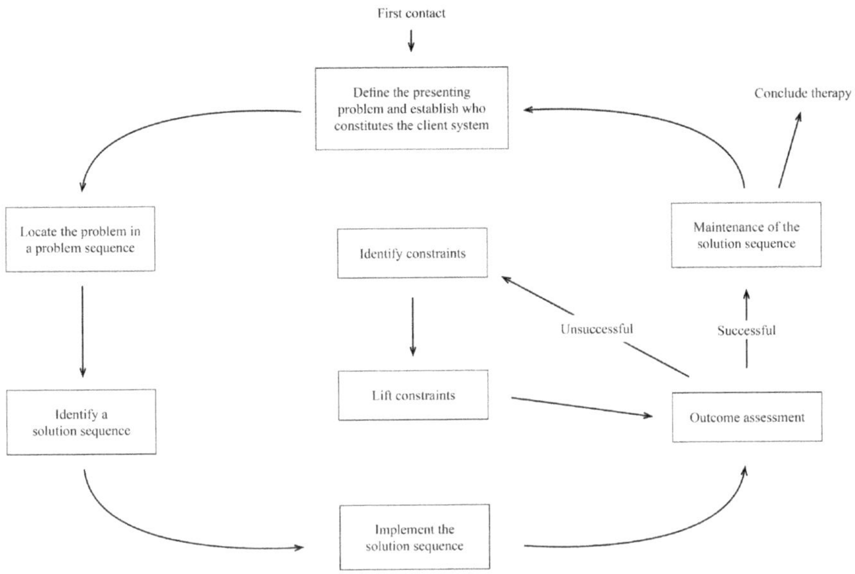

Figure 3.2 The Essence Diagram of Problem Solving

The first step concerns *intake*. The therapist clarifies and *defines the presenting problem* and *establishes who constitutes the client system*, that is, who is directly or indirectly involved in maintaining or resolving the problem (Pinsof et al., 2018; Whittaker & Lorås, 2023). The next step involves *locating the problem in a problem sequence*, the patterned interactions through which the problem is enacted and maintained. In family therapy, these often emerge as recurring behavioral cycles such as unresolvable arguments or conflicts around routines like mealtimes, bedtimes, household responsibilities, or screen use. However, sequences also encompass intrapersonal processes, such as intense shame that triggers avoidance or frustration that precipitates acting-out behavior. For example, a teenager who feels excluded at school may begin to withdraw at home, eliciting parental worry and increased control, which in turn amplifies the adolescent's sense of isolation. In Integrative Systemic Therapy (IST), the perspective is that intrapersonal and interpersonal sequences are inextricably linked.

Once the relevant sequences are mapped within time and context, the therapist and clients collaboratively *identify a solution sequence*, a desired alternative pattern of interaction or experience that can replace or modify the problematic one. Selection of interventions within IST follows the IST guidelines (Pinsof et al., 2018): beginning with the least intrusive, most cost-effective, and most proximal strategy likely to promote change.

Empirically informed methods are favored, yet the process remains fundamentally collaborative and adaptive, guided by the clients' meaning-making and feedback (Tilden & Whittaker, 2022). For example, in the case of a depressed teenager, therapy may initially target the family's attachment behavior to enhance parents' responsiveness and the adolescent's sense of safety and belonging.

After the *implementation of the solution sequence* and if the *outcome is assessed* as successful, the focus of the final phase of therapy shifts toward *maintenance of the solution sequence* before moving to another presenting problem or on to *termination*. If, however, progress is blocked or improvement remains insufficient, IST introduces the concept of *identifying and lifting constraints* (Breunlin, 1999; Pinsof et al., 2018).

A constraint refers to any condition within or surrounding the client system that limits the implementation of adaptive solutions. Constraints can occur at any systemic level, within the individual, between partners or family members, or across larger systems such as the local community, public institutions, or even civilization as a whole. To organize and locate potential constraints, IST employs *the web of human experience* (Figure 3.3; also referred to as *the web of constraints*), a biopsychosocial mapping tool. This tool illustrates how multiple systems intersect to influence both problem maintenance and potential change (Pinsof et al., 2018; Tilden & Whittaker, 2022). The web of human experience integrates systemic levels with the hypothesizing metaframeworks, which encompass key theories relevant to human experience, including *organization*, *development*, *culture*, *biology*, *gender*, *mind*, and *spirituality* (Breunlin et al., 2011; Pinsof et al., 2018).

The web of human experience enables therapists and clients to collaboratively explore what constitutes a given constraint and to identify where it is situated within or adjacent to the client system. Although the web of human experience is introduced here, the hypothesizing metaframework will be discussed in greater detail in Chapter 4, where we examine theories central to understanding child and adolescent development and well-being.

Returning to the example of a depressed teenager introduced previously in this chapter: despite progress in family sessions, the teenager remained socially isolated at school. In this case, the constraint is located at the community level, indicating that meaningful change requires actions beyond the family system, potentially involving teachers, peers, school counselors, or other adults in the adolescent's daily context. Addressing this constraint may involve advocacy, coordination, and systemic outreach, temporarily expanding the therapeutic system to include elements of the youth's broader environment. Once the negative influence of the constraint is sufficiently reduced, for example, by improving school inclusion, the original solution sequence can be reattempted. In some cases, removing the

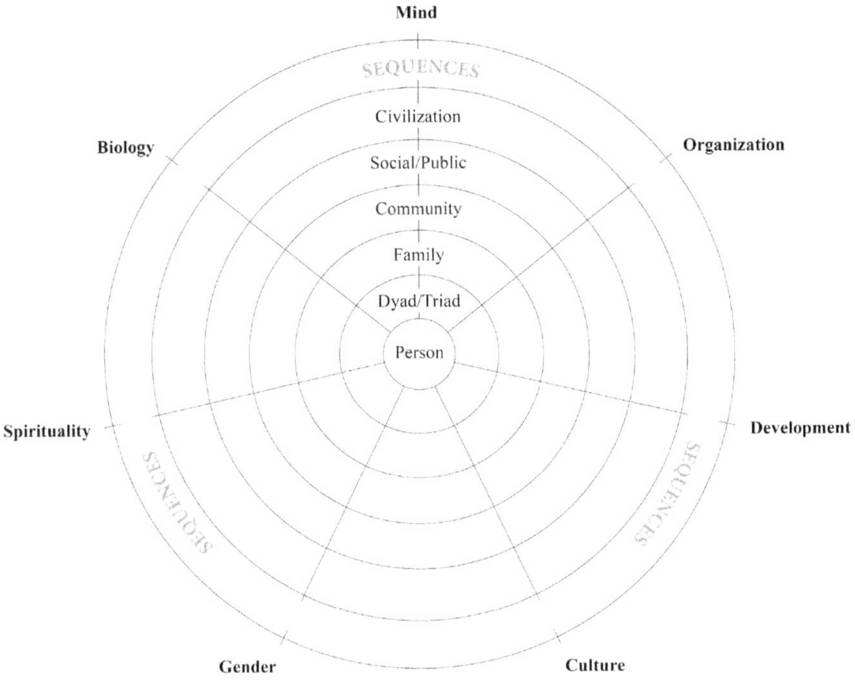

Figure 3.3 The Web of Human Experience

constraint directly resolves the problem, making further intervention unnecessary.

To help locate constraints, the integrative systemic therapist typically poses constraint questions (Pinsof et al., 2018). These questions are worded to identify what gets in the way, such as: *What stops you from attending school?* or *What hinders your understanding of your daughter?* Constraint questions differ from typical motivational questions, which focus on what clients *could* do, for example, *What else could you do, or what could someone do for you, to make it easier to attend school?* When therapy is not progressing as hoped, motivational questions may inadvertently evoke hopelessness, as clients have often already attempted to solve their problem, both on their own and collaboratively in therapy, without success. A common response in such situations is *I have tried that, but things are still the same.*

Motivational questions rest on the assumption that clients are capable of solving their problem but have not yet mobilized the necessary effort or strategy. In contrast, *constraint theory* (Breunlin, 1999) begins with the assumption that clients are *constrained* from solving their problems. The task is therefore not to increase effort, but to identify *what* the constraints are constituted of and *where* in the family or extended system they are located. By uncovering these constraints, therapy aims is to make the resources of the client system accessible again, so that they can be mobilized toward problem resolution.

In summary, working with constraints in IST is, in practice, the same as working with problem sequences. Whether the focus is on implementing a solution sequence or lifting the constraint that prevents its realization, the process remains hypothesis-driven and collaborative. This continuous cycle of hypothesizing, intervening, and evaluating feedback, as illustrated by the blueprint, continues until adaptive change occurs. Once a constraint has been lifted, the therapist and clients may return to implementing the original solution sequence. In some cases, the act of lifting the constraint may itself resolve the problem or alter it sufficiently to meet the clients' goals and conclude treatment. The essence diagram therefore offers therapists a coherent yet flexible structure for navigating the complex multilevel web of human experience and helping clients move from constraint toward connection, competence, and well-being.

The 12 IST guidelines

The 12 Integrative Systemic Therapy (IST) guidelines serve to support decision-making during therapy. The guidelines inform the integrative systemic therapist on how to use the blueprint, the essence diagram, and the web of human experience as well as the hypothesis and planning metaframeworks. The 12 guidelines are as follows: (1) the problem-centered guideline, (2) the strength guideline, (3) the assessment and intervention "inseparability" guideline, (4) the sequence replacement guideline, (5) the empirically informed guideline, (6) the educational guideline, (7) the cost-effectiveness guideline, (8) the interpersonal guideline, (9) the failure-driven guideline, (10) the temporal guideline, (11) the alliance-priority guideline, and (12) the social justice guideline.

1. The problem-centered guideline

To sustain focus on what is essential during the course of therapy and facilitate the therapeutic alliance, the therapist attends closely to the clients' presenting concerns (Pinsof et al., 2018). Problems are understood as unfolding within recurring sequences of behaviors, thoughts, and emotions. Mapping such problem sequences helps clarify the nature of the difficulties and offers an initial systemic understanding of how the clients' concerns are maintained over time. In Integrative Systemic Therapy (IST), problem-solving is therefore understood as an iterative process consisting of a set of tasks aimed at resolving the clients' presenting difficulties as embedded within a recurring sequence. These tasks include convening a client system, defining the problem, contextualizing it within a problem sequence, attempting to modify the sequence or replace it with a solution sequence, identifying constraints to the more adaptive sequence, and removing those constraints (Russell et al., 2023).

2. *The strength guideline*

Integrative Systemic Therapy (IST) is rooted in the understanding that clients' experience of problem-solving can be applied to related or future problems. This assumption informs the strength guideline. The strength guideline states that an extended client system already contains the resources needed to manage life challenges but is constrained from making use of them to resolve current difficulties (Pinsof et al., 2018). This highlights the importance of identifying and removing constraints.

3. *The assessment and intervention "inseparability" guideline*

Integrative Systemic Therapy (IST) makes no differentiation between assessment and intervention. Rather, the process of exploring and understanding the problem is itself understood as potentially therapeutic and may, in some instances, partially or fully alleviate the presenting difficulty. This guideline is also connected to constraint theory, as therapists remain attentive to possible constraints whenever attempts to alter the problem sequence do not lead to meaningful progress (Pinsof et al., 2018).

4. *The sequence replacement guideline*

The goal of Integrative Systemic Therapy (IST) is to replace the problem sequence with a solution sequence—a more constructive and adaptive pattern of behavior. Complete replacement of the problem sequence is not always achievable. However, meaningful therapeutic progress may still occur when the sequence is altered sufficiently to reduce its intensity, frequency, or impact, thereby alleviating the clients' distress (Pinsof et al., 2018).

5. *The empirically informed guideline*

The integrative systemic therapist draws upon knowledge and clinical skills informed by a broad range of research traditions (He et al., 2023). For example, Integrative Systemic Therapy (IST) incorporates findings from common factors research (Sprenkle et al., 2013) as well as empirically informed treatment approaches (e.g., Carr, 2024). Because IST is an integrative and evolving framework, therapists are encouraged to engage in ongoing professional development and remain informed about developments in psychotherapy research. Without such knowledge, therapists may struggle to adapt treatment effectively to the needs of the client system.

6. *The educational guideline*

Within Integrative Systemic Therapy (IST), therapists are encouraged to adopt an active and educative role, sharing knowledge and clinical experience when this is considered helpful and when clients are receptive to it (Pinsof et al., 2018). This may involve taking initiative during therapy, offering guidance, and being appropriately direct when needed. Consequently, IST may be less compatible with therapists who strongly prefer a nondirective therapeutic style that avoids offering suggestions or psychoeducation (He et al., 2023). At the same time, providing knowledge or guidance does not diminish the collaborative nature of therapy, provided that therapists continue to recognize clients as experts on their own lived experience. Indeed, confidence in the therapist's competence has been identified as an important common factor associated with positive therapeutic outcomes (Wampold & Imel, 2015; Whittaker & Tilden, 2025).

7. *The cost-effectiveness guideline*

The cost-effectiveness guideline holds that therapists should begin with the simplest, most direct, and least resource-intensive interventions before considering more complex, indirect, or costly alternatives (Pinsof et al., 2018). Prioritizing interventions that are as efficient and minimally burdensome as possible benefits clients, whether therapy is privately financed or covered through insurance. It may also help safeguard public resources in tax-funded healthcare systems. When financial efficiency aligns with what is therapeutically helpful, it becomes not merely good practice but an ethical commitment to responsible care.

8. *The temporal guideline*

The temporal guideline emphasizes intervening as directly as possible in the clients' current patterns of interaction and behavior. Consequently, integrative systemic therapists typically adopt an action-oriented stance with a primary focus on present-day processes and experiences. Therapeutic work therefore usually begins in the here-and-now and only shifts toward more distant past events and less action-oriented interventions when constraints prevent meaningful progress in resolving the presenting problem (Pinsof et al., 2018).

9. *The interpersonal guideline*

The interpersonal guideline proposes that therapy should, whenever possible, begin in the relational context most directly connected to the presenting problem. This will often involve the couple, parent, or family system rather than the individual alone. In line with the problem-centered guideline, those invited into therapy are typically included because they are assumed to play a meaningful role in either maintaining or resolving the presenting problem. Although Integrative Systemic Therapy (IST) generally favors the inclusion of multiple members of the client system, therapy may begin individually when a client feels strongly about doing so and prioritizing the therapeutic alliance entails respecting this preference. Therapy may also begin individually when conjoint sessions are contraindicated, such as in situations involving ongoing domestic abuse (Pinsof et al., 2018).

10. *The failure-driven guideline*

In Integrative Systemic Therapy (IST), therapeutic tasks and between-session "homework" are often framed as experiments rather than tests of success or failure. When such experiments do not produce the desired outcome, this is not understood as therapeutic failure, but as an opportunity to gain a deeper understanding of the client system and what may be constraining progress in therapy. The failure-driven guideline therefore encourages therapists to identify and explore constraints that may be preventing movement toward a solution sequence (Pinsof et al., 2018).

11. *The alliance-priority guideline*

The alliance-priority guideline emphasizes that establishing and maintaining a strong therapeutic alliance should take precedence over the other Integrative Systemic Therapy (IST) guidelines. However, this priority does not extend to situations in which preserving the alliance compromises the effectiveness, integrity, or safety of the therapeutic process, or otherwise contributes to harm within the client system (Pinsof et al., 2018).

12. *The social justice guideline*

The social justice guideline encourages therapists to remain attentive to the broader cultural and societal context in which clients are situated. This includes awareness of clients' memberships in minority, marginalized, or otherwise disadvantaged groups, and how such experiences may influence both the presenting problem and the therapeutic process (Russell et al., 2022).

Concluding remarks

The core concepts and the 12 Integrative Systemic Therapy (IST) guidelines are highly useful in everyday clinical work. They help the integrative systemic therapist stay oriented, both at the broader level of the overall course of therapy and in the moment-to-moment decisions within each session. The guidelines offer a practical way of working systemically while maintaining a steady focus on the presenting problem and how it can be resolved as efficiently as possible. The reader is reminded to revisit this chapter for reference throughout the book.

Self-reflection task

1. How can maintaining a clear problem focus enhance the therapeutic process?
2. What steps can a therapist take when therapy does not progress as anticipated?
3. In what ways can the Integrative Systemic Therapy (IST) guidelines support and guide therapeutic practice?

References

Breunlin, D. C. (1999). Toward a theory of constraints. *Journal of Marital and Family Therapy*, *25*(3), 365–382. https://doi.org/10.1111/j.1752-0606.1999.tb00254.x

Breunlin, D. C., Pinsof, W., & Russell, W. P. (2011). Integrative problem-centered metaframeworks therapy I: Core concepts and hypothesizing. *Family Process*, *50*(3), 293–313. https://doi.org/10.1111/j.1545-5300.2011.01362.x

Carr, A. (2024). Family therapy and systemic interventions for child-focussed problems: The evidence base. *Journal of Family Therapy*, *47*(1). https://doi.org/10.1111/1467-6427.12476

He, Y., Hardy, N. R., Fisher, A. R., & Lokatama, I. (2023). Development of the integrative systemic therapist. *Fokus På Familien* [Focus on the family], *51*(4), 315–331. https://doi.org/10.18261/fokus.51.4.4

Pinsof, W. M., Breunlin, D. C., Russell, W. P., Lebow, J. L., Rampage, C., & Chambers, A. L. (2018). *Integrative systemic therapy: Metaframeworks for problem solving with individuals, couples, and families*. American Psychological Association. https://doi.org/10.1037/0000055-000

Russell, W. P., Breunlin, D. C., & Lofton, H. C. (2023). Integrative systemic therapy: A feedback-driven perspective. *Fokus På Familien* [Focus on the family], *51*(4), 293–314. https://doi.org/10.18261/fokus.51.4.3

Russell, W. P., Breunlin, D. C., & Sahebi, B. (2022). *Integrative systemic therapy in practice: A clinician's handbook*. Routledge.
Sprenkle, D. H., Davis, S. D., & Lebow, J. L. (2013). *Common factors in couple and family therapy: The overlooked foundation for effective practice*. Guilford Publications.
Tilden, T., & Whittaker, K. J. (2022). Using ROM in family therapy. *Journal of Clinical Psychology*, *78*(10), 1973–1985. https://doi.org/10.1002/jclp.23398
Wampold, B. E., & Imel, Z. E. (2015). *The great psychotherapy debate: The evidence for what makes psychotherapy work*. Routledge. https://doi.org/10.4324/9780203582015
Whittaker, K. J., & Lorås, L. (2023). Integrativ Systemisk Terapi som tilnærming i arbeid med sammensatte problemer. *Fokus på familien* [Focus on the family], *4*(50), 332–348. https://doi.org/10.18261/fokus.51.4.5
Whittaker, K. J., & Tilden, T. (2025). Fellesfaktorer i par og familieterapi [Common factors in couple and family therapy]. In L. Lorås & O. Ness (Eds.), *Håndbok i familieterapi* [Handbook in family therapy] (pp. 83–97). Fagbokforlaget.

Chapter 4

Conversing with Children and Adolescents

Alliance as the Foundation in Therapy

Introduction

Alliance is commonly understood as the quality of the bond between therapist and client, characterized by a shared understanding of therapeutic goals and collaboration on the means to achieve them (Whittaker & Tilden, 2025). Decades of psychotherapy research have consistently shown that alliance is among the most powerful common factors influencing therapeutic outcome, transcending treatment models and client populations (Wampold & Imel, 2015). As one of these core common factors, alliance provides a reliable foundation for change regardless of theoretical orientation. Within Integrative Systemic Therapy (IST), alliance is viewed not only as a dyadic bond but also as a multilayered relational process that extends across the different systems of the family and the broader social contexts in which the child is embedded.

From a family systems perspective, alliance reflects a dynamic balance between three basic processes: the need for belonging, the striving for individuality, and the family's responses to stress or threat (Priest & Lorås, 2026). Families continuously recalibrate these processes to sustain stability and cohesion. Thus, when a child enters therapy, their sense of safety and willingness to engage are closely tied to whether the therapeutic relationship resonates with these systemic needs. In this sense, alliance is built and negotiated not only with the child but also within the child's wider family system.

IST emphasizes that alliances are plural. This systemic conceptualization of the alliance includes not only the therapist's alliance with each family member but also alliances between family members, as well as family members' assessment of each other's alliance with the therapist, and their shared alliance with the therapist and therapist system (Pinsof et al., 2018). Hence, the therapist monitors and adjusts connections across multiple layers throughout the therapeutic process. A strong alliance with the child may lose its effectiveness if parents feel excluded or mistrusted. Conversely, an exclusive parental

DOI: 10.4324/9781003645337-5

alliance may leave the child feeling unseen and unsupported. The central task is therefore to cultivate and balance alliances with all members of the family system, fostering trust, validating each family member's position, and enabling collaborative problem-solving (Whittaker & Tilden, 2025).

This chapter focuses on alliance building with children and adolescents, while recognizing that these alliances are always situated within a family system. Thus, throughout this chapter, the Miller family will serve as a case example to connect theory and practice. Living in a suburban context in Westfield, New Jersey, Rachel and David are raising their two children, Emily (15) and Jacob (9). They are navigating the challenges of adolescent depression, sibling rivalry, and contrasting parental approaches to care.

Alliance and the child's voice

Alliance with children and adolescents depends on how deeply they experience therapy as genuinely collaborative. Collaboration is not a formality but the condition under which trust is created. Children engage when they see that their perspectives shape the direction of therapy, and they withdraw when their contributions go unacknowledged or remain without consequence. Such patterns of engagement and withdrawal reveal that collaboration is not only interpersonal but fundamentally systemic. Within Integrative Systemic Therapy (IST), collaboration is conceptualized as a relational phenomenon that extends beyond the therapist–child dyad. What a child chooses to disclose, the freedom with which they speak, and the meanings they assign to their experiences are always embedded in the family system (McAdam et al., 2022).

From a family systems perspective, collaboration requires attending to both the child's and the parents' needs, which are sometimes complementary and sometimes in tension (Priest & Lorås, 2026). Children may express individuality by asking to speak privately or by withholding sensitive details, yet they still long for the reassurance that their family ties remain intact. Parents, by contrast, often provide clarity, guidance, or solutions while simultaneously wishing to shield their child from further strain. These differing perspectives can create moments of friction. The therapist's role is to move fluidly between them, slowing down when a child hesitates, clarifying expectations when parents press for answers, and creating opportunities where each family member feels included. It is this responsiveness in the moment that turns potential conflict into a balanced collaboration.

One clear expression of such responsiveness is the therapist's flexibility in shaping the session itself. Sessions may take place in the office, on a walk, or through creative media such as drawing or digital tools. These adjustments signal respect for the child's autonomy and comfort, while also showing parents that the process is tailored to their child's needs. What might appear as minor practical changes, such as switching from a table to a couch, shortening session length, or introducing drawing materials, often carry symbolic weight. They demonstrate that the therapist is willing to adapt, and that the child's preferences matter. Research on alliance as a common factor highlights precisely this interplay: when specific methods are embedded in a context of collaboration and respect, they become effective (Whittaker & Tilden, 2025). This same responsiveness also applies to how the therapist handles questions of confidentiality and information sharing.

Therapists therefore need to make explicit agreements that clarify what will be kept private and what will be shared. It is often clinically appropriate to address questions of confidentiality and information sharing directly in the presence of both the child and the parents, so that expectations about what may or may not be shared are clear to all parties. Doing so can help establish transparency from the outset and model a collaborative stance in which the child's voice is explicitly valued. By clarifying how information will be handled while parents are present, the therapist can reduce uncertainty, prevent misunderstandings, and strengthen trust within the therapeutic system. The following example illustrates how such transparency may be articulated in practice:

> Emily, since we are all sitting here together, I want you to know that you are the one who knows best what it feels like to be you. I would really like to hear your perspective. But if something feels too personal, or if you don't want to talk about it right now, you of course do not have to answer any question. Some things may need to be discussed as a family so that we can understand each other better, but we will first talk together about how that could happen and decide collaboratively what feels right to share.

At the same time, children may sometimes speak more freely when parents are not present. In many cases, it can therefore be helpful to have a conversation individually with the child in order to ensure that the child can speak openly and without fear of immediate consequences. During such an individual conversation early in therapy, the therapist might say:

> Emily, you are the one who knows best what it feels like to be you. I would like to hear your perspective, and we will decide together what to share with your parents. Some things may need to be discussed as a family, but you and I will talk first about how that happens.

As shown in the two examples earlier, such statements communicate trust, clarify boundaries, and strengthen the therapeutic alliance. They give the child an active role in shaping the therapeutic process while reassuring parents that important issues will not be ignored but handled carefully. In this way, the child's individuality is respected, and their belonging within the family is preserved (McAdam et al., 2022). Collaboration also extends to siblings, who may otherwise risk feeling invisible when parental concerns center on specific difficulties. Inviting younger siblings into brief, age-appropriate exchanges, such as asking what they miss in their sibling relationship, acknowledges their position in the family and may help prevent escalation through acting out. Even simple acknowledgments can validate their place in the family conversation.

These considerations also have implications for how therapy sessions are structured. At times, a shift from one therapeutic context to another, for example, from family sessions to individual sessions, may be necessary due to safety concerns. More often, however, meeting parents and children separately for one or several sessions serves the purpose of establishing and maintaining the therapeutic alliance (Pinsof et al., 2018). At the same time, seeing members separately, even temporarily, requires careful reflection. A recurring difficulty is that a client may disclose information that is important for other family members to know, but that the therapist cannot use in subsequent sessions if the client wishes to keep it confidential. There is also a risk that a client may share information that the therapist cannot or should not hold alone, as this may later damage the therapist's relationship with other family members if the information emerges later in the therapeutic process. Thus, while shifting between individual and joint sessions can strengthen the alliance, it also requires clear boundaries and thoughtful judgment. It further requires transparent communication about how information will be handled to preserve trust across the family system. While these structural considerations are important, alliance ultimately becomes visible in the small, concrete negotiations that unfold during sessions.

Alliance with children and adolescents is more than listening. It involves ensuring that listening translates into concrete collaboration. When children see that their input shapes the session agenda, and when parents recognize that their concerns are meaningfully integrated into the process, trust grows on both sides. Alliance thus becomes not merely a relational bond, but an ongoing practice of co-creating therapeutic change.

VIGNETTE

During an early session, the therapist asks Emily:

Therapist: "Emily, what would make it a little easier for you to come here and talk?"

Emily: "If we don't always sit at the table. I just feel stuck there."

Therapist: "I see. Can you tell me more about what feels stuck when we sit at the table?"
Emily: *[shrugs]*"I don't know . . . it feels too serious, like I'm in trouble."
Therapist: "That makes sense. Would sitting on the couch, or maybe walking while we talk, make it easier?"
Emily: *[nods]* "Yeah, that feels better."

By adjusting the format based on Emily's feedback, the therapist demonstrates genuine curiosity about her preferences and communicates that her voice has a shaping influence on the process. Collaboration here is not symbolic but enacted in concrete choices, and the alliance strengthens through this simple negotiation (Tilden & Vrabel, 2021). What emerges from this seemingly small shift is characteristic of alliance-building with children. As Øvreeide (2009) emphasizes, children communicate not only through words but also through the conditions they accept for engaging in conversation. Emily's preference for a less formal setting signals her need for safety and relational closeness. By acknowledging and respecting this, the therapist conveys that her lived experience matters. The alliance is therefore not established through abstract assurances but through practical accommodations that allow the child to sense collaboration in action. In this way, collaboration lays the foundation for the next step in strengthening the alliance: moving from validating the child's voice to recognizing and mobilizing their inherent resources and capacities.

Alliance through validation of children's inherent resources and goodness

In accordance with the Integrative Systemic Therapy (IST) strength guideline, the alliance is strengthened when therapists listen to children's struggles while also recognizing their inherent resources (Pinsof et al., 2018). Children bring with them initiative, vitality, and the capacity to positively influence others (Kvello, 2021; Øvreeide, 2022). When these qualities are highlighted, therapy offers a mirror that reflects more than symptoms, allowing the child to see themselves as a competent actor in relationships. This recognition fosters agency and deepens the therapeutic alliance.

Within IST, helping children experience themselves as resourceful connects directly to the systemic processes of belonging and individuality (Priest, 2025). Belonging is nurtured when children feel that their positive contributions matter to their family. Individuality is strengthened when one's unique qualities are noticed and valued. From an IST perspective, validating children's strengths does not mean ignoring problems, but balancing recognition of difficulties with attention to constructive capacities. This balance reduces defensive responses and opens space for collaborative conversations.

Emily's depression often overshadowed the strengths she displayed in daily life. When she entered the therapy room, she appeared withdrawn, her shoulders slumped, and her voice barely audible. At the same time, small moments revealed her resources. She helped Jacob with his homework, comforted a friend through text messages, and prepared tea for her mother after a long day. These gestures carried relational weight. As Øvreeide (2022) notes, even subtle actions can be powerful indicators of how children continue to contribute to their relational contexts. When the therapist noticed and verbalized these contributions, Emily's sense of self shifted from being "the problem" to being an agent with value.

The therapist sometimes drew attention to these moments in conversation with Emily, saying, "Even when you describe having so little energy, I notice you still find ways to support your brother and your friends. How do you think they see you when you do that?" Such recognition validated Emily's resources while inviting her to reflect on her impact. This was not superficial praise, but a systemic intervention that repositioned Emily in relation to her family and peers. As Øvreeide (2009) argues, children's vitality grows when their actions are seen as meaningful contributions to others, and in therapy this recognition becomes a foundation for strengthening the alliance.

Jacob's role also illustrated how children's resources could be central to alliance-building. His acting-out behavior often appeared disruptive. However, behavior is always communicative (Christiansen, 2023). Behind Jacob's protests lay a longing for connection with his sister. When the therapist acknowledged this by saying, "Jacob, it sounds like you really miss Emily. What do you miss most about her?" his energy was reframed as care. Validation shifted him from opposition into collaboration.

Family systems theory highlights that children's vitality is never expressed in isolation but always within a network of relationships (Priest & Lorås, 2026). Emily's care for Jacob strengthened her sense of belonging in the sibling subsystem, while Jacob's persistence affirmed his individuality as someone who refused to be invisible. The therapist's task was to notice these dynamics and make them visible so that the alliance rested not only on understanding difficulties but also on amplifying existing strengths.

When David reacted critically to Emily's withdrawal, the therapist guided the conversation by saying,

> David, I hear how worried you are, and I understand that this sometimes comes out as frustration. At the same time, I have noticed how Emily continues to show care. Could we pause to look at a time when Emily showed that she cared?

This intervention simultaneously strengthened the alliance with both Emily and David. Emily felt that her father was invited to see her more fully, while

David experienced that his concern was acknowledged and redirected toward recognition rather than criticism. This dual alliance illustrates the systemic nature of therapeutic relationships, where validation is distributed throughout the family system (McAdam et al., 2022).

The value of recognition over criticism was also evident when Jacob interrupted a session. As Emily spoke, he blurted, "She never plays with me anymore!" Instead of framing this as disruptive, the therapist responded, "Jacob, I hear you saying you miss playing with Emily. What part do you miss the most?" His expression softened as he said, "She's my sister. I just want her back." Turning to Emily, the therapist asked, "What is it like for you to hear Jacob say that?" Emily replied, "I didn't know it mattered that much to him." What began as an interruption became a moment of recognition, where Jacob's protest was reframed as care and Emily's value affirmed. These exchanges illustrate how alliances form when therapists actively notice and amplify children's relational strengths. Emily's depression narrowed her self-image, but Jacob's expressed longing helped her reconnect with a more vital sense of herself. Jacob learned that his need for closeness could be spoken rather than acted out. For their parents, witnessing such exchanges revealed strengths in their children that might otherwise remain hidden beneath symptoms.

Validating resources is, therefore, not an optional supplement to therapy but an essential aspect of building sustainable alliances (Husby, 2023). By grounding alliance in children's everyday expressions of care, resilience, and vitality, therapists lay the foundation for the next step, which involves bringing these strengths into triadic conversations where multiple family voices are integrated (Øvreeide, 2023).

Alliance in triadic conversations

Alliance is actively shaped in triadic conversations, where children, parents, and siblings participate together. Within Integrative Systemic Therapy (IST), such conversations are central because relationships are understood as the primary context of meaning (Lorås & Whittaker, 2026). When several voices are present and respected, alliance expands beyond the individual child and becomes a shared relational achievement.

At the same time, triadic conversations are also where alliance is most vulnerable (Priest, 2025). Children may hesitate to speak openly in front of their parents, fearing correction, disappointment, or withdrawal of support. Parents may feel torn between the wish to listen and the impulse to protect or instruct. Children's trust, and thereby their alliance with therapy, grows when they experience adults who can receive their words without rushing to explain or correct them (Øvreeide, 2023). The therapist's central task is therefore to safeguard the alliance by creating a predictable frame, regulating the tempo of the conversation, and ensuring that each participant feels genuinely heard (Lorås, 2021).

From a systemic perspective, triadic conversations activate the family's balance between belonging and individuality (Priest & Lorås, 2026). Alliances are strengthened when children can express their individuality without losing their sense of belonging. For a child like Emily, her sense of belonging was secure with her mother, Rachel, but her individuality felt fragile in relation to her father, David. Speaking in front of him risked criticism, which could trigger the family's threat response and weaken the therapeutic alliance. The therapist's goal was to mitigate this threat response, allowing the alliance to create a safe space for vulnerability. This dynamic was visible when Emily tried to address her father. She whispered, "I feel tired all the time. And when I try to explain, I think you see me as lazy." David leaned forward, ready to defend himself. In that moment, the alliance is at risk of breaking down. Instead of letting his reaction dominate, the therapist safeguarded the alliance by asking David to repeat what he had heard. His tone softened as he said, "You feel tired, and you think I see you as lazy." By guiding the conversation, the therapist ensured that Emily's words landed without dismissal, and the alliance between father and daughter was strengthened in that moment.

Triadic conversations also revealed how Rachel's protectiveness could both support and strain the alliance. Her closeness with Emily created comfort, yet speaking on her daughter's behalf undermined Emily's own voice. When Rachel interrupted with, "She's been so exhausted lately, she barely gets out of bed in the morning," Emily sighed and withdrew. The therapist paused, gently acknowledging Rachel's care while inviting Emily to speak for herself. Emily's trembling words, "I just feel like I let everyone down," brought tears to her mother's eyes. Here, the alliance deepened not only between Emily and the therapist but also between Emily and Rachel, as recognition replaced overprotection.

Jacob, at the age of 9, tested the alliance in various ways. His noisy protests risked being dismissed as disruption, yet they also signaled longing for connection. During one session, he exclaimed, "She never laughs anymore!" which Emily received as criticism. The therapist reframed this protest to preserve the alliance, asking Jacob to share a memory of Emily's laughter. He recalled playing soccer in the backyard when Emily had laughed uncontrollably after he fell in the grass. Emily, surprised, whispered, "I didn't think he noticed." By transforming protest into recognition, the alliance the therapist extended the alliance to the sibling relationship, showing Jacob that his longing could be voiced without conflict.

These examples illustrate that systemic alliance is more than a series of parallel bonds between the therapist and each family member. Alliance emerges in the relational space where perspectives are slowed, guided, and reframed. In the Miller family, triadic conversations gradually shifted from fragile interactions to meaningful exchanges. Emily risked saying more, David discovered that listening could be a form of care, Rachel learned to step back, and Jacob realized that his needs could be voiced directly. In this way, the therapeutic alliance became a collective resource, strengthening the family system as a whole. Thus, collaboration in triadic conversations shows that alliance is not only about creating safety for individual voices but about weaving those voices together into a shared process of recognition, belonging, and change.

Alliance when emotions escalate

Within Integrative Systemic Therapy (IST), emotional outbursts are often understood as surface expressions of deeper emotional states related to memories of past painful experiences. They signal where relationships are strained and where the need for recognition is most acute. A child's sense of safety in these moments depends on whether adults and the therapist can contain strong emotions without silencing the child's voice (Øvreeide, 2009). Supporting children to express themselves in manageable ways allows them to remain active participants in shaping the conversation rather than disappearing into the intensity (Kvello, 2021). From a systemic perspective, containment also reduces the family's threat response, where defensive reactions might otherwise dominate and close down communication (Priest & Lorås, 2026).

Conflict in therapy is therefore not a sign of failure but an expected part of systemic work. What matters is how conflict is processed. When intensity is held in ways that sustain both belonging and individuality, it becomes a context for recognition rather than rupture (Russell et al., 2023). Alliance grows as children's individuality is respected while their belonging is safeguarded by parents who remain engaged and emotionally present.

This principle became visible in the Miller family, where escalation often centered on Emily's depression. David interpreted her withdrawal as laziness and voiced frustration, while Rachel countered protectively. For Emily, these conflicting responses reinforced her fear of being a burden. When she whispered, "I feel like I'm failing him. Like I'll never be good enough," the therapist intervened to ensure her words were heard. Instead of responding defensively, David repeated what he had heard, which shifted his stance from judgment to recognition. What could have been a rupture instead became a moment of repair, demonstrating how intensity, when carefully contained, can deepen alliance rather than break it.

The same dynamic appeared in Rachel's overprotective responses. Her care provided a sense of belonging, yet her tendency to speak for Emily undermined her daughter's individuality. By gently pausing and inviting

Emily to share her own experience, the therapist shifted the alliance from substitution to recognition. When Emily, with tears in her eyes, said, "I just feel like I let everyone down," Rachel responded with a softened tone that deepened their alliance as mother and daughter. From a systemic perspective, this shows that alliance is strengthened when parents and children recalibrate positions of voice, care, and recognition in the midst of escalating emotions.

Jacob's outbursts further revealed how children's strong emotions can signal unmet needs for belonging. His protest, *Nobody cares about me!*, could have been dismissed as disruptive, but the therapist reframed it as longing for connection with his sister. When Jacob said, "I just want her back," Emily realized that his anger expressed grief rather than rejection. This shift turned conflict into communication and extended the alliance to the sibling subsystem. From an IST perspective, such moments show how emotional intensity activates systemic patterns of belonging, individuality, and threat response. The therapist's task is to regulate these processes so that each voice remains present and recognized within the larger conversation (Lorås & Whittaker, 2026). For the Millers, what had felt like breaking points became turning points. Emily discovered that her vulnerability could be met with care, David experienced that listening conveyed concern more effectively than criticism, Rachel found she could support without overshadowing, and Jacob learned that his longing could be voiced and acknowledged. In this way, escalation became a pathway through which alliance deepened and the family system was strengthened.

Concluding remarks

Building alliance with children and adolescents is a relational process that unfolds where vulnerability meets recognition, extending beyond the dyadic bond between therapist and child to encompass the family system as a whole. Within Integrative Systemic Therapy (IST), alliance is understood as both fragile and renewable, continuously renegotiated in every meeting and redefined through each interaction. It grows when children experience that their voices carry weight, when parents discover that listening can be a form of care, and when families realize that even strong emotions can be contained without rupture.

From a systemic perspective, alliance represents a dynamic balance between belonging and individuality, two core processes in family life (Priest & Lorås, 2026). Children need to feel anchored in the family system while simultaneously experiencing that their unique perspectives are acknowledged and valued. Thus, alliance deepens when therapy creates conditions that honor both parties in moments of conversation. In this sense, alliance is not a static quality but an emergent property of the family therapist system, continually shaped by patterns of interaction, emotional regulation, and recognition.

For therapists, this means staying attuned to the subtle signals that invite connection (Lorås et al., 2023), whether it is a glance, a sigh, a protest, or a quiet act of care. These signals are not peripheral details but the very material through which alliance is constructed. Responding to them with sensitivity communicates to children and families that their contributions matter, and that the therapeutic space is one where every voice has potential significance. Thus, alliance is about sustaining a horizon where belonging and individuality can grow side by side, offering children the experience of being both seen and valued. It is also about guiding families to discover that their most fragile moments, whether marked by escalation, silence, or misunderstanding, can become openings for deeper recognition. In this sense, alliance is not simply an element of therapy but the thread that weaves together the systemic process of change, carrying families forward into new ways of relating and living with one another.

Self-reflection task

1. How does a therapist show a child or teenager that their voice truly matters in therapy, and why is this important for building trust?
2. How can a therapist balance the needs of parents and children so that everyone feels included and respected?
3. Why might moments of emotional conflict in a family be seen as opportunities for connection and growth rather than signs of failure?

References

Christiansen, J. C. V. (2023). Fem grunnleggende antagelser om kommunikasjon [Five basic assumptions about communication]. In F. Thuen & L. Lorås (Eds.), *Lærebok i kommunikasjon* [Textbook in communication] (pp. 44–60). Fagbokforlaget.

Husby, V. (2023). *Målbevisst ferdighetstrening* [Purposeful skills training]. Gyldendal.

Kvello, Ø. (2021). *Samtaler med barn og ungdom. Medvirkning, kommunikasjon og metoder* [Conversations with children and adolescents. Involvement, communication and methods]. Fagbokforlaget.

Lorås, L. (2021). Systemiske spørsmål i relasjonelle samtaler [Systemic questions in relational conversations]. In L. Lorås & J. C. V. Christiansen (Eds.), *Samtaler i relasjonelt arbeid* [Conversations in relational work] (pp. 81–92). Fagbokforlaget.

Lorås, L., Christiansen, J. C. V., & Lindeman, S. (2023). Systemisk, sosialkontruksjonisme og meningskoordinering som perspektiver på kommunikasjon [Systemic, social constructionism and coordinated management of meaning as perspectives of communication]. In L. Lorås & J. C. V. Christiansen (Eds.),

Samtaler i relasjonelt arbeid [Conversations in relational work] (pp. 19–32). Fagbokforlaget.
Lorås, L., & Whittaker, K. J. (2026). Integrative systemic therapy. In O. Smoliak, E. Tseliou, T. Strong, S. Bava, & P. Muntigl (Eds.), *The Routledge international handbook of postmodern therapies* (pp. 249–262). Routledge.
McAdam, E., Lang, P., Henoa, D., & Lorås, L. (2022). *The protective interview. Releasing the tangled web of incest.* Taos Institute publications.
Øvreeide, H. (2009). *Samtaler med barn- metodiske samtaler med barn i vanskelige livssituasjoner* [Conversations with children—methodical dialogues with children in difficult life situations]. Cappelen Damm Akademisk.
Øvreeide, H. (2022). Barns godhet [Children's goodness]. *Fokus på Familien* [Focus on the family], *4*(50), 274–290. https://doi.org/10.18261/fokus.50.4.2
Øvreeide, H. (2023). Samtaler med barn og ungdom—et triadisk prosjekt [Conversations with children- a triadic project]. In L. Lorås & J. C. V. Christiansen (Eds.), *Samtaler i relasjonelt arbeid* [Conversations in relational work] (pp. 93–124). Fagbokforlaget.
Pinsof, W. M., Breunlin, D. C., Russell, W. P., Lebow, J. L., Rampage, C., & Chambers, A. L. (2018). *Integrative systemic therapy. Metaframeworks for problem solving with individuals, couples and families.* American Psychological Association. https://doi.org/10.1037/0000055-000
Priest, J. (2025). *The science of family systems theory.* Routledge.
Priest, J., & Lorås, L. (2026). *Familiesystemteori. Teori, evidens og praksis* [Family systems theory. Theory, evidence and practice]. Fagbokforlaget.
Russell, W. P., Breunlin, D. C., & Lofton, H. C. (2023). Integrative systemic therapy: A feedback-driven perspective. *Fokus på Familien* [Focus on the family], *4*(50), 293–314. https://doi.org/10.18261/fokus.51.4.3
Tilden, T., & Vrabel, K. A. (2021). Fellesfaktorer i psykoterapi [Common factors in psychotherapy]. In P. E. Binder, L. Lorås, & F. Thuen (Eds.), *Håndbok i individualterapi* [Handbook in individual therapy] (pp. 89–104). Fagbokforlaget.
Wampold, B. E., & Imel, Z. E. (2015). *The great psychotherapy debate: The evidence for what makes psychotherapy work.* Routledge. https://doi.org/10.4324/9780203582015
Whittaker, K. J., & Tilden, T. (2025). Fellesfaktorer i par og familieterapi [Common factors in couple and family therapy]. In L. Lorås & O. Ness (Eds.), *Håndbok i familieterapi* [Handbook in family therapy] (pp. 83–97). Fagbokforlaget.

Chapter 5

The Hypothesizing Metaframeworks as they Relate to Children and Adolescents

Introduction

Working with children and adolescents in therapy requires knowledge that extends beyond what is typically needed when working with adults. In Integrative Systemic Therapy (IST), this knowledge is organized through the hypothesizing metaframeworks, visualized in the web of human experience (Figure 3.3). Building on the systemic principles outlined in Chapter 2, the hypothesizing metaframeworks help therapists organize patterns of interaction and key dimensions of family functioning into clinically useful competencies. Each of the seven metaframeworks in IST refers to a family of related theories, namely culture, development, biology, mind, gender, spirituality, and organization (Pinsof et al., 2018). No single metaframework is sufficient to fully explain a family system's presenting problem, its possible solutions, or the constraints that limit access to problem-solving resources. Instead, therapists apply multiple, complementary lenses to develop a sufficiently rich description of the client system.

Over the past century, our knowledge of the development of children and adolescents has increased enormously. At the same time, children have increasingly been recognized as full members of society. Childhood is now perceived as a valuable part of life, laying the very foundation as to how we live and function as adults. The rights of the children as stated in the UN convention (Convention on the Rights of the Child, 1989) serve to protect children and adolescents, granting them the right to have a childhood and to experience well-being and protection. However, many still experience adversity. There is a considerable symptom burden experienced globally by today's youth (Piao et al., 2022). The distress experienced by children and adolescents is influenced by a myriad of factors including genetic vulnerabilities, premature or traumatic births, neglect, abuse or other adverse events, social exclusion, and bullying. Not only is there a risk of maladaptive development, but expected development also has its risks as adolescents strive to form their identities and find their place in adult society,

DOI: 10.4324/9781003645337-6

while at the same time, navigating an ever more complex world influenced by digital technologies, social media, and politics.

Although some metaframeworks may perhaps seem more relevant than others, all of the seven metaframeworks may be utilized when considering the lives and struggles of children and adolescents. Within each metaframework, we review selected theories that shed light on the types of presenting problems encountered in clinical practice with children, adolescents, and their families. For the sake of readability, we have chosen to separate each of the metaframework's constituent theories into classical and contemporary perspectives. The aim is not to provide an exhaustive overview, but to encourage the reader to use the IST hypothesizing metaframeworks as a flexible tool when supporting young clients and their families.

Culture metaframework

The culture metaframework encompasses the shared social practices, norms, institutions, and systems of meaning through which human societies organize life, including knowledge, beliefs, arts, laws, and customs (Jahoda, 2012). Cultural contexts play a central role in shaping children's and adolescents' development and identity formation. At the same time, children and adolescents are not passive recipients of culture; they actively co-construct their own cultures through play, learning, and peer interaction. This is particularly evident in adolescence, a developmental period marked by increasing autonomy from the family and a growing orientation toward peer-group belonging and social identity (Corsaro, 1992).

Classical perspectives

There have been some defining works written during the 20th century which have highlighted how culture affects the development of children and adolescents. For example, Margaret Mead's *Coming of Age in Samoa* (1928) concluded that adolescence in Samoa was not associated with the emotional distress, as observed in industrialized societies. Urie Bronfenbrenner's *The Ecology of Human Development* (1979) introduced a systemic framework for understanding how multiple cultural contexts such as family, school, and overall society shape the development of the child and adolescents. Further, Super and Harkness's concept of the developmental niche (1986, 2002) suggested how the interaction of child-rearing practices, parental psychology, and societal norms creates the environments in which children develop. Altogether, these frameworks make the compelling argument that development is not only biological or psychological but is always situated in cultural contexts.

Contemporary perspectives

A wide range of studies (Gielen & Roopnarine, 2016) have shown that children's and adolescents' cultures differ significantly across the world. This makes cultural sensitivity essential for therapists. Awareness is needed not only toward the members of the dominant culture but also, perhaps with greater urgency, toward the experiences of minority groups. Self-esteem and identity are often negotiated within minority cultures, and therapists must attend to these dynamics. The concept of intersectionality (Crenshaw, 1989) highlights how overlapping identity markers such as ethnicity, gender, and social class shape children's and adolescents' experiences. For example, second-generation immigrants may live according to their parents' traditions at home while appearing indistinguishable from peers in the dominant culture at school. For many, adapting to multiple environments is seamless; for others, it can be strenuous. How caregivers evaluate their children's belonging to different cultural contexts also matters. Do they support their adolescents' participation in the dominant youth culture, or perceive it as a threat to family values and traditions? Understanding these questions is crucial for systemic work with families.

A description of the influence of culture today would be incomplete without considering social media. Perhaps the biggest difference between those raised before the 2010s and those growing up today is the presence of online platforms. Most adolescents, and even some younger children despite age restrictions, have one or more social media accounts. Although research shows both positive and negative impacts on adolescents' mental health from social media use (Valkenburg et al., 2022), it has become almost a compulsory activity if one wants to participate fully in social life. Social media has its own languages, symbols, and rituals, and serves as a space where children and adolescents may seek advice or support from peers, for better or worse. Studies have highlighted risks, such as links between excessive use and self-harm, depressive symptoms (Vidal et al., 2020), risky behavior (Vannucci et al., 2020), and bullying (Ang, 2015). Yet it is equally important to acknowledge the positive potential of online spaces, where young people can feel connected and supported, and experience heightened well-being (Best et al., 2014).

To understand today's youth, both the classical and contemporary perspectives need to be considered. Children and adolescents may be members of more than one culture, and these cultures are not static but evolving. An effective therapist thereby needs to consider the cultural contexts that children and adolescents move through, including their homes, schools, peer groups, as members of minority or majority cultures, and increasingly online. Only then can young people be understood and provided with appropriate help.

Development metaframework

Although all development frameworks may be applied, developmental psychology is of particular importance when working with children and adolescents. It is a field which spans domains such as sensory and motor development, language, cognition, and identity formation. There is natural overlap with the biology metaframework, since both address processes of growth and maturation. In this section, however, we emphasize areas most closely related to how caregivers support a child's development and well-being. Within Integrative Systemic Therapy (IST), developmental challenges and goals are not viewed as individual matters, but as processes embedded in relational and systemic sequences (Pinsof et al., 2018; Russell et al., 2023).

Classical perspectives

Many theories of cognitive and emotional development have been presented during the last century, and perhaps one of the most influential ones is Piaget's theory of cognitive development (1962). Through his observational studies, Piaget observed how children moved through distinct stages of reasoning, developing more abstract and formal ways of thinking as they aged and matured. Another important theorist of the 20th century was Erikson. Erikson's theory of psychosocial development of identity (1968) proposed that identity was something that developed across stages as the person grappled with mastering set challenges. For example, the tasks to master as an adolescent are related to social and academic skills. The associated virtue the adolescent may potentially integrate because of this mastery is one of competency. Perhaps one of the most influential developmental theories for the present-day field of family therapy is Bowlby's attachment theory (1988). Bowlby highlighted how infants are born hardwired to bond with caregivers, and how these relationships play a key role in shaping relational expectations and emotional regulation. Attachment theory has become hugely influential, not only in family therapy but also within many fields of psychotherapy, underpinning many contemporary psychotherapy models (e.g., emotionally focused therapies [Gottman & Gottman, 2015; Johnson, 2012] and psychodynamic therapies [e.g., Davanloo, 2001]). Together, these theories provide a foundation for understanding developmental tasks and vulnerabilities, and they remain influential in systemic practice when assessing how developmental challenges manifest within families.

Contemporary perspectives

As research has progressed, so have the classical theories been revised and extended, and newer theories have emerged. Mentalization theory proposes that infants develop their capacity to understand their own and others' mental states through engagement with their caregivers. Severe disturbances in this process may lead to psychopathology (Fonagy, 2003). Conversely, resilience research demonstrates how supportive relationships and adaptive coping strategies can mitigate against adversity (Masten, 2013). Advances in affective neuroscience have further uncovered how the developing brain is shaped by early relational experiences in infancy to achieve adequate emotional regulation later in life (Schore, 2021).

A particularly influential discovery in neuroscience has been that of mirror neurons (Rizzolatti & Craighero, 2004). These brain neurons are active both when a person performs actions and when they observe others perform them, making them central to imitation, empathy, and social learning. Mirror neurons provide a biological foundation for processes such as mentalization, attachment, and emotional regulation. They help explain how infants and children learn language, acquire skills, and develop an understanding of their own and others' feelings. For integrative systemic therapists, awareness of mirroring processes can also be clinically useful, for example, by observing how children and parents unconsciously mirror each other's expressions or affect in session. Such moments of attunement or misattunement can become entry points for therapeutic intervention.

Two central concepts in developmental psychopathology are equifinality and multifinality (Cicchetti & Rogosch, 1996). They shed light on the complex and often surprising interactions of nature and nurture. Equifinality refers to how different starting points or experiences may lead to the same developmental outcome. In contrast, multifinality refers to how similar experiences may lead to very different outcomes. These concepts may be of use when trying to understand why a child's developmental outcome is not as expected. For example, two children with dyslexia may face very different futures. If one child is identified early and provided with appropriate support, the likelihood of positive academic and psychosocial development increases. If another child with the same challenge goes unnoticed, difficulties are likely to accumulate, leading to poorer outcomes in life. Similarly, a child who grows up with secure attachment does not automatically establish secure adult relationships but is more likely to do so than a peer with disorganized attachment, a pattern often linked to neglect and trauma and associated with difficulties in adolescence and adulthood.

Although equifinality and multifinality are hypothetical constructs, they are nonetheless valuable for clinicians. They remind us to examine why some children experience less optimal development while others appear more resilient, even when their life experiences seem contradictory. Vygotsky's concept of the zone of proximal development (1978) complements this line of thinking by showing how children, when supported by parents, teachers, or peers, can achieve developmental goals that would otherwise be out of reach. Bandura's social learning theory (1977) adds another layer by emphasizing how children acquire new skills and behaviors not only by direct interaction with others but also through observing and modeling others in their environment.

These perspectives align with Integrative Systemic Therapy's (IST) systemic orientation, underscoring the importance of relationships and contexts in shaping development (Pinsof et al., 2018). They remind therapists that individual capacities should not be viewed in isolation but as emerging within relational, familial, cultural, and contextual environments (see also Rogoff, 2003).

Biology metaframework

The biology metaframework draws upon theories that many family therapists may be less familiar with than those typically encountered in the social sciences. This area is often perceived as belonging primarily to medical doctors and other professionals concerned with the biological aspects of human functioning. However, it is useful for the integrative systemic therapist to have a working knowledge of biological perspectives. Biological processes provide the foundation upon which psychological, developmental, and relational patterns emerge, and thus they are integral to a systemic understanding of children and adolescents. It is also important for therapists to understand how illness in family members may influence the therapeutic process. Concepts from biology such as genetics, heredity, and evolutionary adaptation are central to understanding human well-being as well as physiological and psychological development.

Classical perspectives

Perhaps the most important contributions to our modern understanding of human development came from Darwin's theory of evolution. His observations presented in *On the Origin of Species* (1859) laid the groundwork for understanding human adaptation and the field of behavioral genetics that would follow. Chess and Thomas (1977) illustrated how biologically based individual differences shape children's responses to their environments. Such differences in temperament are the basis of what we later in life recognize as personality traits.

Early studies of brain trauma also underscored the importance of biology for psychological functioning including personality (Harlow, 1849, 1993; Gazzaniga & Sperry, 1967). Studies of critical periods in brain and sensory development demonstrated that certain functions must be established during specific windows of time if they are to develop normally (Cisneros-Franco et al., 2020), illustrating how biological processes early in life are crucial for later functioning.

Contemporary perspectives

Modern approaches to study brain development, although building upon the concepts of specialized brain regions and critical periods in brain development, would demonstrate how children's brains are able to reorganize in response to stress and learning. This phenomenon is called neuroplasticity and refers to the brain's capacity to adapt throughout a human's lifespan (Kolb & Gibb, 2014). Although many breakthroughs within the field of genetics have occurred, a crucial one for our understanding of the relationship between nature and nurture is what is known as epigenetics. Epigenetics refers to how gene expression can be altered by environmental influences, including trauma and caregiving quality (Meaney, 2010). With the discovery of epigenetics, man is no longer beholden to a deterministic view of gene expressions but is given the power to influence how certain genes are turned "on" or "off." These findings underscore Integrative Systemic Therapy's (IST) systemic emphasis on constraints and sequences, showing how biological vulnerabilities and strengths are expressed differently depending on relational, environmental, and cultural contexts.

From a therapy perspective, several concepts regarding the nervous system are particularly relevant. For example, research regarding the hypothalamic–pituitary–adrenal (HPA) axis helps explain how children adapt to or are overwhelmed by adversity (Gunnar & Quevedo, 2007). Another related work is Porges and Furman's polyvagal theory (2011). Polyvagal theory has shaped our understanding of how the vagus nerve, which is a cranial nerve connected to the parasympathetic nervous system, is involved in emotional and cognitive processing. The interplay between the vagus nerve and the parasympathetic nervous system regulates capacities such as perception of safety, social engagement, and co-regulation. For therapists, awareness of these processes and how they are affected by stress, interpersonal or otherwise, can inform how they observe regulation and dysregulation in children and families, and how co-regulation in the therapeutic relationship can support stabilizing a family system or facilitate change.

Finally, the integrative systemic therapist working with adolescents should have knowledge of pubertal development. The sex hormones involved are estrogens for girls and testosterone for boys; these hormones drive the biological changes seen in puberty. Not only are they involved in these biological changes but they also profoundly influence adolescents' emotions, risk-taking behavior, and family dynamics (Berenbaum et al., 2015). Changes in the body also provoke questions related to identity including gender identity (see the gender metaframework). Recognizing these underlying biological processes allows therapists to understand developmental transitions more clearly and to support families in navigating them.

Both the classical and contemporary perspectives show that biology is not separate from relational life but a constant part in shaping it, and vice versa. For integrative systemic therapists, understanding biological processes provides an essential foundation for appreciating how children and adolescents grow, adapt, and sometimes struggle within their families and wider contexts.

Mind metaframework

The mind metaframework is among the most conceptually rich, as it draws upon theories concerning emotion, cognition (including memory), meaning-making, the development of self, and even the nature of consciousness. This metaframework also incorporates an element of time, understood as a subjective experience. Perception of time is not limited to memory and sequencing of past events, but may also be altered in ordinary situations, for example, moments of deep absorption or flow, when time seems to pass differently. It may also shift in distressing states such as traumatic flashbacks or disorientation in dementia. In this section, we will primarily focus on processes of emotion, cognition, and meaning-making as they emerge in the here-and-now of therapeutic work.

Classical perspectives

Several foundational theories have shaped our understanding of the relationship between emotions and cognition. The James–Lange theory (Dewey, 1894) suggested that bodily reactions to environmental stimuli occur first, and that emotions arise from the interpretation of these reactions. Ekman (1992) identified what he proposed to be six universal emotions expressed across cultures, emphasizing the biological basis of affect. Beck's cognitive model (1979) described how situations trigger automatic thoughts that in turn generate emotional responses. Izard's differential emotions theory (1977) proposed that discrete emotions serve adaptive functions throughout development.

Although distinctions between emotion and cognition are often made, these differences are largely conceptual, and debates typically focus on the sequence in which they occur. Beck's model suggests that cognition precedes emotion, while James–Lange implies that bodily reactions come first. Attributing sadness to crying rather than crying to sadness may sound counterintuitive, yet it underscores the role of brain maturation, interpretation, and states of consciousness in shaping emotional experience. For instance, a child may sometimes cry without knowing why and only later be able to explain with the help of a caregiver. At other times, the opposite may be true: the child clearly knows the reason for the tears. Hence, more than one theory may apply depending on the context. For therapists, these classical perspectives remain useful for understanding how children express and interpret emotions, reminding us that developmental stage and individual differences strongly influence how feelings are experienced and communicated in therapy.

Contemporary perspectives

Our understanding of how cognition and emotions manifest has advanced significantly over the past several decades due to developments in brain imaging and statistical modeling (Lindquist et al., 2012). One influential contribution is Barrett's theory of constructed emotion (2017). While classical theories tended to classify emotions into discrete categories (e.g., sadness, anger, contempt, disgust, enjoyment, fear, and surprise; Ekman, 1992) linked to specific brain regions (i.e., the limbic system), Barrett's theory takes a different stance. It proposes that emotions are constructed predictions: networks of neural activity throughout the brain draw upon past experiences to anticipate what is about to happen and to prepare an adaptive response. The felt experience of this prediction is what we call emotion. This perspective implies that how we construe meaning from our environments and internal states depends heavily on prior experiences. In development, children learn from caregivers, family members, and peers which cues are important to respond to, underscoring the highly relational and social nature of emotions.

Contemporary views of cognition have also moved away from concepts of discrete categories, toward understanding thought processes as fluid and context-dependent. Within cognitive neuroscience, dynamical systems theory (Favela, 2020) has been applied to understand thoughts and ideas as self-organizing processes embodied in sensory and motor behavior and dependent on context. In this view, cognition is emergent and fluid, with new expressions of behavior arising through the interaction of neural, bodily, and relational systems. Although not originally developed within family therapy, this perspective resonates with systemic thinking: Therapists may observe how children's thoughts and behaviors shift in session as emergent outcomes of relational dynamics. This framing underscores how meaning and cognition are continuously co-constructed in the interaction of neural, bodily, and relational systems.

For an integrative systemic therapist, the priority is to understand how sequences of behavior, emotion, cognition, and meaning-making unfold for a particular client or family, rather than to adhere rigidly to one model of thought and emotion. It is crucial to recognize how intrapsychic sequences both shape and are shaped by relationships, and what implications they may have for the problem sequence or the implementation of the solution sequence. Hence, integrative systemic therapists must consider how constraints and resources influence intrapsychic sequences and how they can be adjusted to support change.

Classical perspectives are helpful for grounding therapeutic models, while contemporary perspectives provide more nuanced accounts of how cognitions and emotions manifest. By integrating both, integrative systemic therapists can remain flexible and adaptive, tailoring interventions to a child or adolescent's developmental stage, individual differences, and systemic context. This integrative approach enables therapists to support children and adolescents in ways that honor both development and its contextual complexities.

Gender metaframework

The gender metaframework draws attention to how gender identity, roles, and expectations influence the development of children and adolescents and their relationships within the family. At the same time, these patterns are shaped by the broader social and cultural contexts in which young people grow up. For most children and adolescents, discovering their biological sex and developing a gender identity is a natural part of growing up. In many Western contexts, young people are increasingly exposed to a range of perspectives on gender. This exposure enables opportunities to explore identities that extend beyond traditional associations between biological sex and gender. However, for some, this process can be painful and confusing, particularly when societal or familial expectations conflict with personal experience. Even for those who identify as cisgender, gender expectations can sometimes be experienced as limiting or difficult. The gender metaframework becomes relevant both when addressing such difficulties and when normalizing common developmental experiences related to gender, such as undergoing puberty or navigating intimacy and sexual development. Within the web of human experience, gender intersects with several metaframeworks and multisystemic levels, including biological processes, identity development and sense of self, relational dynamics within families and peer groups, and broader cultural expectations.

Classical perspectives

Early theorists, including Freud (1961), emphasized sex differences and traditional roles when discussing gender. Social learning theories (Bem, 1981; Bussey & Bandura, 1984) highlighted the importance of modeling and reinforcement, suggesting that children learn gender roles by observing others and receiving feedback from caregivers and their community. Other theorists, such as Kohlberg (1966), proposed that children actively construct their gender identity through a sequence of stages, gradually acquiring constancy and stability of gender identity. These perspectives laid the foundation for later, more nuanced understandings of gender, while also reflecting the cultural assumptions of their time.

Contemporary perspectives

In recent years, questions concerning the relationship between biological sex and gender identity have become widely discussed in both clinical and public discourse, particularly in debates surrounding transgender identities and approaches to gender-affirming care. For some, these discussions echo earlier debates about homosexuality, when questions of pathology versus normality dominated. Increasingly, however, contemporary theories emphasize that gender is socially constructed, fluid, and intersecting with other identity markers such as culture, social class, and ethnicity (Butler, 2002; Crenshaw, 1989). Drawing upon developmental psychology, research shows how children and adolescents actively negotiate gender norms within their peer groups and families (Martin & Ruble, 2010). For therapists, this means that gender must be understood in relation to culture, family systems, and broader social structures.

For integrative systemic therapists, it is important to attend to how the child or adolescent and their family talk about and make sense of gender in everyday life and in therapy. These conversations may reveal potential constraints or resources related to gender norms, expectations, and roles that influence the presenting problems and the therapeutic process. Gender norms can limit opportunities, shape family expectations, and contribute to distress when a child or adolescent does not conform to them. Gender norms may also influence how authority, responsibilities, and resources are distributed within families, for example, in relation to leadership and decision-making, caregiving responsibilities, and access to economic opportunities. At the same time, gender identity and expression can be sources of resilience, belonging, and pride. Attending to the social justice guideline of Integrative Systemic Therapy (IST) helps therapists act as supportive allies to children and adolescents, regardless of their biological sex or gender identity.

Spirituality metaframework

For many therapists, the spiritual domain is not considered when practicing therapy. In Integrative Systemic Therapy (IST), however, the whole of human experience is encompassed, and therefore both resources and possible constraints regarding spirituality need to be considered when relevant. Within the spirituality metaframework, one finds literature and knowledge of practices related to religion, spirituality, awe-inspiring experiences, and philosophical or existential questions.

Classical perspectives

Spirituality and religion have long been central to human life and identity. Early psychological theories such as the one presented in William James's book *The Varieties of Religious Experience* (1902) emphasized the role of spiritual practices and mystical states in shaping well-being. Later, existential thinkers like Viktor Frankl (1959) highlighted the search for meaning as a fundamental human drive, often expressed in spiritual or philosophical terms.

Contemporary perspectives

In modern psychology and therapy, spirituality is increasingly studied as a resource for coping, resilience, and identity development. Studies have shown that children and adolescents may draw on religious or spiritual frameworks to find meaning during illness, loss, or transitions (Elzamzamy et al., 2024). Research suggests that spirituality in adolescence is relatively stable over time and positively associated with prosocial behavior and well-being (Kor et al., 2019). Spirituality may also have a protective role in preventing depression and anxiety in adolescence (Aggarwal et al., 2023). Conversely, spiritual or religious traditions can also become sources of conflict when beliefs clash within families or between families and broader society. Contemporary perspectives emphasize respecting diversity of traditions while also attending to how power and exclusion may operate through religious or spiritual norms.

Spiritual themes may impact children and adolescents in multiple ways: through their own beliefs or interests, the beliefs of their parents, the religious expectations of their community, or a personal search for meaning. Sometimes a therapist may already know about a client's faith and tradition, which can help them to better understand the client's situation. At other times, access to knowledge about someone's beliefs is minimal. In such circumstances, it is especially important for the therapist to navigate with humility and respect. In some cases, it may be helpful to draw upon a third party with special knowledge of a particular faith tradition. This can be done indirectly (i.e., seeking out relevant knowledge), or with consent, such as inviting a knowledgeable third party to participate in the session. For an integrative systemic therapist, the goal is not to provide spiritual guidance but to recognize how spirituality may function as either a resource or a constraint within the family system and to support the child's or adolescent's own meaning-making.

Organization metaframework

The organization metaframework refers to theories about boundaries and leadership. Concepts of boundaries and leadership are relevant to many areas, including teamwork, organizations, professional life, and family life, as they influence structure, motivation, collaboration, and the management of complex relationships and diverse perspectives.

Classical perspectives

Within family therapy, the most influential theorist to address leadership, hierarchy, and boundaries was Salvador Minuchin. In his pioneering work on structural family therapy (1974), he focused on several core concepts such as coalition, enmeshment, and hierarchy in the family system. Coalitions refer to situations in which two or more family members align against another member of the family, for example, when a mother and her children band together to chastise the father, or when teenagers unite against a single parent, creating structural imbalances within the family system. Enmeshment refers to a weakening of boundaries between subsystems, which can lead to unhealthy relationships and rigid interaction patterns. For instance, an overprotective mother or father may unintentionally inhibit her or his child's development. The concept of hierarchy highlights the role of the parental subsystem. When the parental subsystem functions well, it provides leadership and clear decision-making that ensures children are adequately cared for. When the parental subsystem is weakened or dysfunctional, children or adolescents may assume leadership responsibilities beyond their level of maturity. Such disturbances in the family hierarchy may lead them to behave in ways that appear older than their biological age would suggest, often in an effort to compensate for weaknesses in the parental subsystem. Conversely, family members may at times assume roles or behaviors that are not developmentally typical for their biological age. Minuchin's ideas have been central in shaping how family therapists understand organizing processes within families and remain relevant for Integrative Systemic Therapy's (IST) systemic practice today.

Contemporary perspectives

Since the 1980s, postmodern and constructivist thinkers have critiqued the rigid application of hierarchy and fixed roles in families (e.g., Goldner, 1985). They emphasized that leadership within families is not static but negotiated and flexible, shifting according to developmental stages, context, and cultural values. Rather than assuming a fixed parental authority, these perspectives highlight shared and interactive aspects of leadership and collaborative decision-making, where authority can be distributed among family members depending on situation and need (Boston, 2000). This shift reflects a broader movement in therapy toward valuing dialogue, negotiation, and co-construction of roles over prescriptive models of family organization.

For integrative systemic therapists, the organization metaframework highlights the importance of assessing how boundaries and leadership function within families. These processes are closely related to the balance between belonging and individuality within the family system. Problems may arise when boundaries are too diffused or too rigid, or when the parental leadership is weakened. Therapeutic work can involve strengthening the parental subsystem, clarifying boundaries, and helping family members find healthier patterns of collaboration. At the same time, therapists should be attentive to how leadership can be shared and renegotiated, supporting families in creating flexible structures that allow for both stability and adaptability. This is especially important when working with children and adolescents, who gradually gain more independence and leadership over their own lives as they grow up.

Concluding remarks

Understanding and helping children and adolescents is inherently complex. Therapy is at its best when theoretical knowledge covering the whole of human experience is applied. This involves drawing on theories of development, biology, culture, gender, organization, mind, and spirituality when relevant. As highlighted in this chapter, none of these metaframeworks stand alone; they are best used together to explain how they shape both well-being and distress. As noted, the sections covering each of the seven metaframeworks are not exhaustive but are intended as a starting point. As cases become more complex, therapists may need to explore certain metaframeworks in greater depth, applying them flexibly to support the needs of children, adolescents, and their families.

Self-reflection task

1. How might the hypothesizing metaframeworks enhance your understanding of a family?
2. Which of the metaframeworks do you anticipate using most frequently in your own practice, and why?
3. Are there any metaframeworks that you believe are missing or insufficiently represented?

References

Aggarwal, S., Wright, J., Morgan, A., Patton, G., & Reavley, N. (2023). Religiosity and spirituality in the prevention and management of depression and anxiety in young people: A systematic review and meta-analysis. *BMC Psychiatry*, *23*(1), 729. https://doi.org/10.1186/s12888-023-05091-2

Ang, R. P. (2015). Adolescent cyberbullying: A review of characteristics, prevention and intervention strategies. *Aggression and Violent Behavior*, *25*, 35–42. https://doi.org/10.1016/j.avb.2015.07.011

Bandura, A., & Walters, R. H. (1977). *Social learning theory*. Prentice Hall.

Barrett, L. F. (2017). The theory of constructed emotion: An active inference account of interoception and categorization. *Social Cognitive and Affective Neuroscience*, *12*(1), 1–23.

Beck, A. T. (1979). *Cognitive therapy and the emotional disorders*. Meridian. https://doi.org/10.1093/scan/nsx060

Bem, S. L. (1981). Gender schema theory: A cognitive account of sex typing. *Psychological Review*, *88*(4), 354. https://doi.org/10.1037/0033-295x.88.4.354

Berenbaum, S. A., Beltz, A. M., & Corley, R. (2015). The importance of puberty for adolescent development: Conceptualization and measurement. *Advances in Child Development and Behavior*, *48*, 53–92. https://doi.org/10.1016/bs.acdb.2014.11.002

Best, P., Manktelow, R., & Taylor, B. (2014). Online communication, social media and adolescent wellbeing: A systematic narrative review. *Children and Youth Services Review*, *41*, 27–36. https://doi.org/10.1016/j.childyouth.2014.03.001

Boston, P. (2000). Systemic family therapy and the influence of post-modernism. *Advances in Psychiatric Treatment*, 6(6), 450–457. https://doi.org/10.1192/apt.6.6.450

Bowlby, J. (1988). *Attachment* (2nd ed.). Basic Books.

Bussey, K., & Bandura, A. (1984). Influence of gender constancy and social power on sex-linked modeling. *Journal of Personality and Social Psychology*, *47*(6), 1292. https://doi.org/10.1037/0022-3514.47.6.1292

Bronfenbrenner, U. (1979). *The ecology of human development*. https://doi.org/10.4159/9780674028845

Butler, J. (2002). *Gender trouble*. Routledge.

Chess, S., & Thomas, A. (1977). Temperamental individuality from childhood to adolescence. *Journal of the American Academy of Child Psychiatry*, *16*(2), 218–226. https://doi.org/10.1016/s0002-7138(09)60038-8

Cicchetti, D., & Rogosch, F. A. (1996). Equifinality and multifinality in developmental psychopathology. *Development and Psychopathology*, *8*(4), 597–600. https://doi.org/10.1017/s0954579400007318

Cisneros-Franco, J. M., Voss, P., Thomas, M. E., & de Villers-Sidani, E. (2020). Critical periods of brain development. In A. Gallagher, C. Bulteau, D. Cohen, & J. L. Michaud (Eds.), *Handbook of clinical neurology: Vol. 173. Neurocognitive development: Normative development* (pp. 75–88). Elsevier. https://doi.org/10.1016/B978-0-444-64150-2.00009-5

Corsaro, W. A. (1992). Interpretive reproduction in children's peer cultures. *Social Psychology Quarterly*, *55*(2), 160. https://doi.org/10.2307/2786944

Crenshaw, K. (1989). Demarginalizing the intersection of race and sex: A Black feminist critique of antidiscrimination doctrine, feminist theory and antiracist politics. *University of Chicago Legal Forum, 1989*(1), 139–167. https://chicagounbound.uchicago.edu/uclf/vol1989/iss1/8/

Davanloo, H. (2001). *Intensive short-term dynamic psychotherapy: Selected papers of Habib Davanloo, MD*. John Wiley & Sons.
Dewey, J. (1894). The theory of emotion: I: Emotional attitudes. *Psychological Review, 1*(6), 553. https://doi.org/10.1037/h0069054
Ekman, P. (1992). Are there basic emotions? *Psychological Review, 99*(3), 550–553. https://doi.org/10.1037/0033-295x.99.3.550
Elzamzamy, K., Naveed, S., & Dell, M. L. (2024). Religion, spirituality, and pediatric mental health: a scoping review of research on religion and spirituality in the journal of the American academy of child and adolescent psychiatry from 2000 to 2023. *Frontiers in Psychiatry, 15*, 1472629. https://doi.org/10.3389/fpsyt.2024.1472629
Erikson, E. H. (1968). *Identity: Youth and crisis*. W. W. Norton & Company.
Favela, L. H. (2020). Dynamical systems theory in cognitive science and neuroscience. *Philosophy Compass, 15*(8), e12695. https://doi.org/10.1111/phc3.12695
Fonagy, P. (2003). The development of psychopathology from infancy to adulthood: The mysterious unfolding of disturbance in time. *Infant Mental Health Journal, 24*(3), 212–239. https://doi.org/10.1002/imhj.10053
Frankl, V. E. (1959). *From death-camp to existentialism: A psychiatrist's path to a new therapy* (I. Lasch, Trans.). Beacon Press.
Freud, S. (1961). Some psychical consequences of the anatomical distinction between the sexes. In J. Strachey (Ed. & Trans.), *The standard edition of the complete psychological works of Sigmund Freud* (Vol. 19, pp. 243–258). Hogarth Press (Original work published 1925).
Gazzaniga, M. S., & Sperry, R. W. (1967). Language after section of the cerebral commissures. *Brain, 90*(1), 131–148. https://doi.org/10.1093/brain/90.1.131
Gielen, U. P., & Roopnarine, J. L. (Eds.). (2016). *Childhood and adolescence*. ABC-CLIO. https://doi.org/10.5040/9798400625176
Goldner, V. (1985). Feminism and family therapy. *Family Process, 24*(1), 31–47. https://doi.org/10.1111/j.1545-5300.1985.00031.x
Gottman, J. S., & Gottman, J. M. (2015). *10 principles for doing effective couples therapy (Norton series on interpersonal neurobiology)*. WW Norton & Company.
Gunnar, M. R., & Quevedo, K. M. (2007). Early care experiences and HPA axis regulation in children: A mechanism for later trauma vulnerability. *Progress in Brain Research, 167*, 137–149. https://doi.org/10.1016/s0079-6123(07)67010-1
Harlow, J. M. (1849). Passage of an iron rod through the head. *The North-Western Medical and Surgical Journal, 1*(6), 513. https://doi.org/10.1056/nejm184812130392001
Harlow, J. M. (1993). Recovery from the passage of an iron bar through the head. *History of Psychiatry, 4*(14), 274–281. https://doi.org/10.1177/0957154x9300401407
Izard, C. E. (1977). *Human emotions*. Plenum Press. https://doi.org/10.1007/978-1-4899-2209-0
Jahoda, G. (2012). Critical reflections on some recent definitions of "culture." *Culture & Psychology, 18*(3), 289–303. https://doi.org/10.1177/1354067x12446229
James, W. (1902). *The varieties of religious experience: A study in human nature*. Longmans, Green, and Co.
Johnson, S. M. (2012). *The practice of emotionally focused couple therapy: Creating connection*. Routledge.
Kohlberg, L. (1966). A cognitive-developmental analysis of children's sex-role concepts and attitudes. In E. E. Maccoby (Ed.), *The development of sex differences* (pp. 82–173). Stanford University Press.

Kolb, B., & Gibb, R. (2014). Searching for the principles of brain plasticity and behavior. *Cortex*, *58*, 251–260. https://doi.org/10.1016/j.cortex.2013.11.012

Kor, A., Pirutinsky, S., Mikulincer, M., Shoshani, A., & Miller, L. (2019). A longitudinal study of spirituality, character strengths, subjective well-being, and prosociality in middle school adolescents. *Frontiers in Psychology*, *10*, 377. https://doi.org/10.3389/fpsyg.2019.00377

Lindquist, K. A., Wager, T. D., Kober, H., Bliss-Moreau, E., & Barrett, L. F. (2012). The brain basis of emotion: A meta-analytic review. *The Behavioral and Brain Sciences*, *35*(3), 121. https://doi.org/10.1017/s0140525x11000446

Martin, C. L., & Ruble, D. N. (2010). Patterns of gender development. *Annual Review of Psychology*, *61*(1), 353–381. https://doi.org/10.1146/annurev.psych.093008.100511

Masten, A. S. (2013). Global perspectives on resilience in children and youth. *Child Development*, *85*(1), 6–20. https://doi.org/10.1111/cdev.12205

Mead, M. (1928). *Coming of age in Samoa: A psychological study of primitive youth for Western civilisation*. William Morrow.

Meaney, M. J. (2010). Epigenetics and the biological definition of gene × environment interactions. *Child Development*, *81*(1), 41–79. https://doi.org/10.1111/j.1467-8624.2009.01381.x

Minuchin, S. (1974). *Families & family therapy*. Harvard University Press.

Piao, J., Huang, Y., Han, C., Li, Y., Xu, Y., Liu, Y., & He, X. (2022). Alarming changes in the global burden of mental disorders in children and adolescents from 1990 to 2019: A systematic analysis for the global burden of disease study. *European Child & Adolescent Psychiatry*, *31*(11), 1827–1845. https://doi.org/10.1007/s00787-022-02040-4

Piaget, J. (1962). *Play, dreams, and imitation in childhood*. W. W. Norton & Company.

Pinsof, W. M., Breunlin, D. C., Russell, W. P., Lebow, J. L., Rampage, C., & Chambers, A. L. (2018). *Integrative systemic therapy: Metaframeworks for problem solving with individuals, couples, and families*. American Psychological Association. https://doi.org/10.1037/0000055-009

Porges, S. W., & Furman, S. A. (2011). The early development of the autonomic nervous system provides a neural platform for social behaviour: A polyvagal perspective. *Infant and Child Development*, *20*(1), 106–118. https://doi.org/10.1002/icd.688

Rizzolatti, G., & Craighero, L. (2004). The mirror-neuron system. *Annual Review of Neuroscience*, *27*(1), 169–192. https://doi.org/10.1146/annurev.neuro.27.070203.144230

Rogoff, B. (2003). *The cultural nature of human development*. Oxford University Press.

Russell, W. P., Breunlin, D. C., & Lofton, H. C. (2023). Integrative systemic therapy: A feedback-driven perspective. *Fokus På Familien* [Focus on the family], *51*(4), 293–314. https://doi.org/10.18261/fokus.51.4.3

Schore, A. N. (2021). The interpersonal neurobiology of intersubjectivity. *Frontiers in Psychology*, *12*. https://doi.org/10.3389/fpsyg.2021.648616

Super, C. M., & Harkness, S. (1986). The developmental niche: A conceptualization at the interface of child and culture. *International Journal of Behavioral Development, 9*(4), 545–569. https://doi.org/10.1177/016502548600900409

Super, C. M., & Harkness, S. (2002). Culture structures the environment for development. *Human Development*, *45*(4), 270–274. https://doi.org/10.1159/000064988

United Nations General Assembly. (1989). *Convention on the rights of the child.* https://www.ohchr.org/en/instruments-mechanisms/instruments/convention-rights-child

Valkenburg, P. M., Meier, A., & Beyens, I. (2022). Social media use and its impact on adolescent mental health: An umbrella review of the evidence. *Current Opinion in Psychology*, *44*, 58–68. https://doi.org/10.1016/j.copsyc.2021.08.017

Vannucci, A., Simpson, E. G., Gagnon, S., & Ohannessian, C. M. (2020). Social media use and risky behaviors in adolescents: A meta-analysis. *Journal of Adolescence*, *79*(1), 258–274. https://doi.org/10.1016/j.adolescence.2020.01.014

Vidal, C., Lhaksampa, T., Miller, L., & Platt, R. (2020). Social media use and depression in adolescents: A scoping review. *International Review of Psychiatry*, *32*(3), 235–253. https://doi.org/10.1080/09540261.2020.1720623

Vygotsky, L. S. (1978). *Mind in society: The development of higher psychological processes.* Harvard University Press.

Chapter 6

The Hypothesis and Planning Matrix

Introduction

As discussed in Chapter 5 on the hypothesizing metaframeworks, children and adolescents, and the families they are part of, experience distress for many different reasons. Throughout this book, our focus is on understanding how family members may either support or inadvertently constrain a child's development and well-being. Because the challenges brought to therapy vary widely, therapists require access to a broad repertoire of ways to help. No single method is suitable for every client, and effective clinical work therefore involves integrating ideas and strategies drawn from multiple therapeutic traditions.

In this chapter, we introduce ways of selecting techniques and methods that may be useful when working with families. In Integrative Systemic Therapy (IST), this task is supported by the hypothesis and planning matrix (Figure 6.1). The matrix integrates the hypothesizing metaframeworks and the planning metaframeworks into a single, unifying conceptual tool. The hypothesizing metaframeworks organize the theories and concepts used to understand children, adolescents, and their families, while the planning metaframeworks bring together knowledge about treatment strategies for addressing identified problems and constraints. Although the hypothesis and planning matrix may initially appear overwhelming, the ability to navigate it provides a clear advantage when selecting appropriate treatment strategies to facilitate therapeutic change.

The hypothesis and planning matrix and its constituent metaframeworks are conceptual tools that help therapists translate working hypotheses into actionable therapeutic plans. This planning process is embedded within the blueprint, which illustrates how therapists determine a treatment strategy based on client feedback and the ongoing refinement of their hypotheses.

As with the chapter on the hypothesizing metaframeworks, this chapter is not intended to be exhaustive, nor does it function as a manual prescribing what therapists should do. Rather, it serves as a guide for how

DOI: 10.4324/9781003645337-7

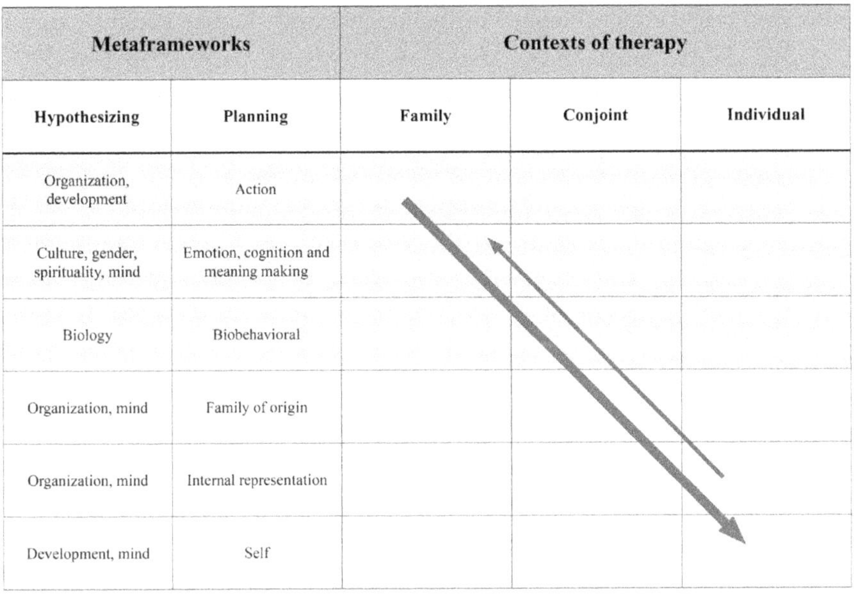

Figure 6.1 The Hypothesis and Planning Matrix

therapists might think about intervening when faced with clinical complexity. Effective therapists must retain the freedom to choose interventions that align with their own way of being. This freedom to select and apply interventions in a manner consistent with one's personality, values, and assumptions about human experience helps therapists come across as competent, genuine, and effective helpers (Wampold & Imel, 2015).

Planning what to do and when to execute

As illustrated in the hypothesis and planning matrix, each hypothesizing metaframework is paired with a corresponding planning metaframework; for example, organizational hypotheses often align with action-oriented interventions. These pairings serve as useful heuristics: constraints identified within a particular hypothesizing metaframework are often most effectively addressed through interventions drawn from the corresponding planning metaframework. However, these pairings should not be understood as prescriptive. Therapists frequently draw on multiple planning metaframeworks in response to evolving case formulations, ongoing client feedback, and an updated understanding of the problem sequence.

Consistent with Integrative Systemic Therapy's (IST) recognition of equifinality in problem-solving, there is no single intervention pathway for resolving a specific problem or lifting a constraint. Rather, multiple strategies may lead to the desired outcome (Pinsof et al., 2018). The therapist's task is therefore to work collaboratively with the client system to identify and implement the intervention strategy that best fits the presenting problem, the context, and the clients' capacities.

Because IST is, at its core, an integrative approach, the selection of interventions is not primarily driven by the assumptions of any single therapeutic model (for example, the idea that a specific psychiatric diagnosis necessarily requires a diagnosis-specific treatment). Instead, clinical decision-making is guided by the metatheory underpinning IST practice, including the IST planning guidelines. Consequently, interventions in IST are selected according to a set of organizing principles rather than adherence to a particular model.

When an intervention fails to modify the problem sequence or reduce an identified constraint, a therapeutic shift becomes necessary. This shift is represented by the large downward-pointing arrow in the hypothesis and planning matrix and may occur either horizontally, reflecting a change in treatment context, or vertically, reflecting a shift in the planning metaframework. A lack of expected progress thus provides valuable feedback about what to do next (i.e., the failure-driven guideline). It may prompt adjustments to the client system, such as including additional family members, or a shift between planning metaframeworks, for example, from action-oriented strategies to interventions focused on emotion, cognition, or meaning-making.

The large downward-pointing arrow in the hypothesis and planning matrix also signifies that change efforts are initially directed toward the here-and-now, addressing current interactional patterns before moving to more distal influences (i.e., the temporal guideline). Most family therapies tend to operate primarily within the upper three planning metaframeworks of the matrix, which address problems and constraints located in the present. Only occasionally do they extend into the lower three metaframeworks, which more commonly organize constraints rooted in the past. For example, a parent's own childhood trauma may be identified as a constraint that inhibits their ability to respond to their child's needs.

The most cost-effective interventions are prioritized, beginning with simpler and more direct strategies before progressing to more complex or resource-demanding approaches (i.e., the cost-effectiveness guideline). The left-to-right orientation of the downward-pointing arrow illustrates therapeutic shifts in treatment context: therapy should begin by involving the appropriate family members whenever feasible and move toward individual sessions only when necessary, due to identified constraints (i.e., the interpersonal guideline). Working within the family context offers several advantages in therapy with children and adolescents, including enhanced parental understanding, opportunities to learn new ways of responding to one another, and the facilitation of healthier interactional patterns among family members.

The small upward-pointing arrow signifies that all interventions must form part of an overarching plan to resolve the presenting problem as it is expressed in the problem sequence (i.e., the problem-focused guideline). Its right-to-left orientation further reflects IST's preference for involving multiple family members in therapy whenever appropriate (i.e., the interpersonal guideline). In addition, the small upward-pointing arrow directs attention toward the action metaframework, underscoring that the resolution of any presenting problem ultimately becomes visible through observable actions or interactions. The educational guideline is also embedded in this arrow, emphasizing that IST is a learning process in which the therapist both teaches and guides clients toward new understandings and skills at a pace that allows for meaningful integration.

The planning guidelines of IST frame therapy as a process of intervening in problem sequences and the constraints that maintain them, while simultaneously helping clients learn how to navigate such challenges more effectively. This requires therapists to tailor their approach to each client system, including making appropriate cultural adaptations and attending to clients' membership in minority or identity groups. Consequently, the integrative systemic therapist is best understood as an expert in the breadth of therapy rather than a specialist in a single therapeutic model. This does not imply that integrative systemic therapists cannot develop mastery in specific approaches. Many will, depending on their professional context. Instead, they continuously update their working knowledge and skill set to meet the diverse and evolving needs of the families they serve (He et al., 2025).

At the same time, IST does not presume that every therapist can help every client. A core clinical responsibility involves recognizing when a case calls for expertise or services that fall outside the therapist's competence or the resources of the clinical setting. When a more intensive or complex intervention strategy is indicated, the therapist initiates an appropriate therapeutic shift. Such shifts may involve referrals, coordination with other service systems, or transitions to treatments that are more specialized, more intensive, or longer in duration. These shifts should not be understood as failures, but rather as a natural and expected aspect of a treatment that prioritizes accurate problem conceptualization, guided clinical decision-making, and client safety.

The planning metaframeworks

The planning of interventions occurs both between sessions, as part of the therapist's ongoing preparation, and spontaneously within sessions in response to client feedback. Although the Integrative Systemic Therapy (IST) planning guidelines offer clear recommendations for how therapy should begin, they are intended to be applied flexibly. It is not always possible, nor clinically advisable, to initiate therapy by implementing interventions from the action metaframework in a multi-person context. For example, an integrative systemic therapist may receive a referral within a specialized setting, such as an inpatient family unit. In such cases, therapy may need to begin within the family-of-origin metaframework, working collaboratively with clients to lift constraints rooted in the past before an adaptive solution sequence can be implemented. Under other circumstances, it may be necessary for the therapist to work with a parent individually, either before or between family sessions. This supports emotional regulation and strengthens the parent's capacity to extend this regulation to their child (Whittaker, 2018).

In the following sections, we review each of the planning metaframeworks, describe representative interventions associated with each, and illustrate their application through a case example.

Action

The action metaframework consists of treatment strategies that target expressed behavior in the here-and-now. For children, this may include family-based behavioral programs, such as interventions addressing bedtime routines and unwanted nighttime waking (Bathory & Tomopoulos, 2017), or interventions for adolescent eating disorders that support parents in managing challenging eating situations (Rienecke, 2017). Other approaches focus more directly on parent–child interactions (e.g., Aarts, 2000; McNeil & Hembree-Kigin, 2010). Additional strategies draw on traditional family therapy techniques, such as paradoxical interventions designed to alter problematic behavioral sequences (Haley, 1987) or enactments (Minuchin, 1974).

Fundamentally, enactment is a technique for deliberately setting up interactions between family members. It is useful not only for directing conversations in session but also for examining problem sequences and implementing solution sequences in vivo. By inviting family members to interact with one another rather than through the therapist, enactments make relational patterns visible and available for therapeutic change.

Enactments are often used in tandem with reframing (described in the emotion, cognition, and meaning-making metaframework). For example, when a child describes feeling frightened when a parent does not respond, the therapist may first reframe the child's experience to highlight its importance and then invite an enactment:

> It sounds like those scary feelings you have when your mother doesn't respond are really important. Do you think your mom knows what that

feels like for you? Would you be willing to tell her about it in your own words right now?

In this way, reframing helps clarify the emotional significance of the experience, while enactment creates an opportunity for direct communication between family members. Together, these interventions allow the therapist to observe interactional patterns as they occur and to support the family in practicing more adaptive ways of relating.

VIGNETTE

In the following vignette, we illustrate how a therapist may implement intervention strategies from the action metaframework to resolve a problem sequence. Troy (11) is referred to therapy with his mother due to his highly selective eating habits. In the early phase of treatment, Troy, his mother, and the therapist make steady progress. Through gradual exposure to new foods and tastes, and with the therapist's support, Troy's mother learns to resist giving in to his protests while maintaining his motivation with appropriate rewards. As a result, Troy begins to expand his diet. In these sessions, the therapist draws primarily on behavioral strategies to address Troy's selectivity directly, while also integrating emotion, cognition, and meaning-making interventions to coach his mother in emotionally attuned parenting that promotes confidence, structure, and warmth.

Although the therapist is aware that Troy does not see his father regularly because he lives in another part of the country, Troy does spend holidays with him. After one such visit, Troy and his mother return to therapy reporting a relapse: Troy has once again begun refusing foods he had previously accepted. In the session that follows, Troy's mother shares her suspicion that Troy's father may have unintentionally undermined their progress. When she confronted him by phone, he acknowledged that he had allowed Troy to eat whatever he preferred during their time together.

As the therapist listens to Troy and his mother, she formulates a hypothesis that the relapse is linked to an organizational constraint, specifically, inconsistency in parental leadership across households. She anticipates that similar setbacks may occur after future holiday visits unless this issue is addressed.

The therapist shares her working hypothesis with Troy and his mother, taking care not to sound critical of Troy's father, and asks for their permission to reach out to him. Troy's mother readily agrees. Troy hesitates, and the therapist notices his expression: he appears protective of his father and understood to lie in the father's own developmental history. A therapeutic shift toward individual-oriented work was therefore initiated.

The therapist arranged a series of online sessions with the father. In these sessions, they explored how aspects of his upbringing and long-standing shame-based responses constrained his capacity for emotional regulation and, in turn, his ability to respond supportively to Troy's emotional distress. Addressing these internal representation and self-related constraints proved necessary for lifting the parental limitations that had been interfering with the implementation of an effective solution sequence for Troy.

Concluding remarks

As demonstrated throughout this chapter, the hypothesis and planning matrix, together with its constituent metaframeworks and the Integrative Systemic Therapy (IST) planning guidelines, provides a coherent structure for a therapeutic process that can be adapted to the needs of each individual family. Interventions are seldom confined to a single planning metaframework; more often, therapists draw flexibly and skillfully on strategies from multiple planning metaframeworks to lift or reduce the constraints most relevant to resolving a presenting problem.

Just as human experience cannot be neatly delineated or compartmentalized, neither can the range of treatment strategies available to the integrative systemic therapist. For this reason, the hypothesis and planning matrix, like all IST tools, should be understood as a flexible guide rather than a rigid prescription. The hypothesizing and planning metaframeworks are not static constructs but dynamic tools. They are continuously refined as new knowledge, therapeutic approaches, and technologies emerge, and as existing practices develop. The overarching aim of IST and its conceptual tools is to support therapists in making responsive, informed, and context-sensitive clinical decisions that ultimately enhance the well-being of their clients.

Self-reflection task

1. How can the hypothesis and planning matrix support therapists in making informed decisions about when to maintain a current intervention strategy and when to initiate a therapeutic shift?
2. What are the potential benefits and limitations of therapeutic approaches that focus on solving problems as they manifest in the here-and-now, compared to approaches that target the historical roots of a problem?

3. Under what clinical circumstances might it be necessary or appropriate to shift from present-focused interventions to strategies that address more distal or historical constraints?

References

Aarts, M. (2000). *Marte Meo: Basic manual*. Aarts Productions.
Anderson, H., & Gehart, D. R. (Eds.). (2012). *Collaborative therapy: Relationships and conversations that make a difference*. Routledge.
Babinski, D. E., & Sibley, M. H. (2021). Family-based treatments for attention-deficit/hyperactivity disorder: A review of family functioning outcomes in randomized controlled trials from 2010 to 2019. *Journal of Marital and Family Therapy*, *48*(1), 83–106. https://doi.org/10.1111/jmft.12572
Bathory, E., & Tomopoulos, S. (2017). Sleep regulation, physiology and development, sleep duration and patterns, and sleep hygiene in infants, toddlers, and preschool-age children. *Current Problems in Pediatric and Adolescent Health Care*, *47*(2), 29–42. https://doi.org/10.1016/j.cppeds.2016.12.001
Bennett, R. S., Denne, M., McGuire, R., & Hiller, R. M. (2020). A systematic review of controlled trials for PTSD in maltreated children and adolescents. *Child Maltreatment*, *26*(3), 325–343. https://doi.org/10.1177/1077559520961176
Claussen, A. H., Holbrook, J. R., Hutchins, H. J., Robinson, L. R., Bloomfield, J., Meng, L., Bitsko, R. H., O'Masta, B., Cerles, A., Maher, B., Rush, M., & Kaminski, J. W. (2022). All in the family? A systematic review and meta-analysis of parenting and family environment as risk factors for attention-deficit/hyperactivity disorder (ADHD) in children. *Prevention Science*, *25*(S2), 249–271. https://doi.org/10.1007/s11121-022-01358-4
Dattilio, F. M. (2010). *Cognitive-behavioral therapy with couples and families: A comprehensive guide for clinicians*. Guilford Press.
Diamond, G. S., Diamond, G. M., & Levy, S. A. (2014). *Attachment-based family therapy for depressed adolescents*. American Psychological Association. https://doi.org/10.1037/14296-000
Furrow, J. L., Palmer, G., Johnson, S. M., Faller, G., & Palmer-Olsen, L. (2019). *Emotionally focused family therapy*. Routledge. https://doi.org/10.4324/9781315669649
Gaskin, C. J., Venegas Hargous, C., Stephens, L. D., Nyam, G., Brown, V., Lander, N., Yoong, S., Morrissey, B., Allender, S., & Strugnell, C. (2024). Sleep behavioral outcomes of school-based interventions for promoting sleep health in children and adolescents aged 5 to 18 years: A systematic review. *Sleep Advances*, *5*(1). https://doi.org/10.1093/sleepadvances/zpae019
Haley, J. (1987). *Problem-solving therapy* (2nd ed.). Jossey-Bass.
He, Y., Hardy, N., Fisher, A., & Venketramen, N. (2025). *Integrative systemic supervision: Training therapists to work with individuals, couples, and families*. Taylor & Francis. https://doi.org/10.4324/9781003146841
Madanes, C. (1991). *Strategic family therapy*. Jossey-Bass
McGoldrick, M. (2016). *The genogram casebook: A clinical companion to genograms: Assessment and intervention*. WW Norton & Company.
McNeil, C. B., & Hembree-Kigin, T. L. (2010). *Parent–child interaction therapy*. Springer. https://doi.org/10.1007/978-0-387-88639-8
Minuchin, S. (1974). *Families and family therapy*. Routledge. https://doi.org/10.4159/9780674041127

Morello, L., Caputi, M., Scaini, S., & Forresi, B. (2022). Parenting programs to reduce recurrence of child maltreatment in the family environment: A systematic review. *International Journal of Environmental Research and Public Health*, *19*(20). https://doi.org/10.3390/ijerph192013283

Pinsof, W. M., Breunlin, D. C., Russell, W. P., Lebow, J. L., Rampage, C., & Chambers, A. L. (2018). *Integrative systemic therapy: Metaframeworks for problem solving with individuals, couples, and families*. American Psychological Association. https://doi.org/10.1037/0000055-009

Rienecke, R. (2017). Family-based treatment of eating disorders in adolescents: Current insights. *Adolescent Health, Medicine and Therapeutics*, *8*, 69–79. https://doi.org/10.2147/AHMT.S115775

Scharff, D. E., & Scharff, J. S. (1987). *Object relations family therapy*. Jason Aronson.

Wampold, B. E., & Imel, Z. E. (2015). *The great psychotherapy debate: The evidence for what makes psychotherapy work*. Routledge. https://doi.org/10.4324/9780203582015

Wang, X., Cai, Z., Jiang, W., Fang, Y., Sun, W., & Wang, X. (2022). Systematic review and meta-analysis of the effects of exercise on depression in adolescents. *Child and Adolescent Psychiatry and Mental Health*, *16*(1). https://doi.org/10.1186/s13034-022-00453-2

White, M., & Epston, D. (1990). *Narrative means to therapeutic ends*. W. W. Norton & Company

Whittaker, K. J. (2018). Flere perspektiver i ett: En introduksjon til integrativ systemisk terapi. *Fokus på Familien*, *46*(3), 180–187 [Focus on the family]. https://doi.org/10.18261/issn.0807-7487-2018-03-03

Part II

Chapter 7

First Contact and Defining the Problem

Introduction

In this chapter, we follow the Peterson family as they meet with their integrative systemic therapist. The Petersons are a White, Lutheran, middle-class family living just outside Decorah, a small town in northeastern Iowa known for its strong Scandinavian heritage, close-knit community, and natural beauty.

Anders (47), the father, grew up in Winneshiek County and has spent most of his life in and around Decorah. Maria (42), the mother, is originally from Chicago and comes from an Italian American family. They have two children: Gia (8) and Jon (5), both of whom attend elementary school and appear generally well adjusted.

Gia enjoys reading, drawing, and working on classroom projects, and she is doing well academically. Jon is active and imaginative, thrives on routines, and enjoys outdoor play, building with blocks, and pretending to be animals or superheroes. Although he functions well both at home and at school, he can become frustrated when asked to shift tasks or share attention, particularly with his sister. Gia maintains a close relationship with both her parents and her brother, but has recently begun to show greater independence, often preferring to spend time on her own or with friends. While her parents are not currently concerned, they remain attentive as she navigates this new developmental phase.

At the time the couple contacts the therapist, Maria is in her third trimester of pregnancy. Given both her and Anders's age, as well as previous complications following childbirth, the couple is experiencing heightened anxiety about the health and development of their unborn child. As a result, they have not yet told Gia and Jon about the pregnancy.

The therapist had previously worked with Anders and Maria early on in their relationship, nearly a decade ago, when they were planning their family. When the therapist recently received their email requesting help, she felt a quiet weight settle in her chest. It was not only the return of

DOI: 10.4324/9781003645337-9

familiar names but also the sense of urgency between the lines. This time, they were not seeking support solely as a couple; they also wanted to bring their children into therapy.

In this chapter, we use the case of the Petersons to illustrate the first steps of the Integrative Systemic Therapy (IST) essence diagram (Figure 3.2): *first contact*, *establishing the client system*, and *defining the presenting problem*. Throughout this early phase of therapy, the therapist uses the blueprint to systematically attend to client feedback, formulate and refine working hypotheses, plan intervention strategies, and enact these through ongoing therapeutic dialogue.

First contact

In Integrative Systemic Therapy (IST), it is crucial to identify who belongs to *the direct client system* and who belongs to *the indirect client system*. The direct client system refers to those who actively participate in therapeutic conversations, whereas the indirect client system includes other family members or significant individuals who are not currently attending therapy. Designation to either the direct or indirect client system is provisional and may change as therapy progresses (Figure 7.1). For example, sessions involving the whole family may be interspersed with sessions with one or both parents to help alleviate constraints affecting their capacity to parent (Breunlin & Jacobsen, 2014; Pinsof et al., 2018).

The therapist knew from the email that both Maria and Anders would be participating and that they had concerns related to the pregnancy, but beyond this the message offered little information. The therapist was particularly interested in whether any other family members would be attending the first session. Reflecting on their previous contact, she imagined that their two children must have grown considerably since the last time Maria and Anders sought help. The therapist therefore realized that she needed to contact them to plan effectively for the initial session and to clarify whether anyone else would be joining.

Convening the direct client system usually entails inviting relevant family members to participate in therapy. This is reflected in the interpersonal guideline, which states that all individuals involved in the presenting problem, or in its resolution, should be invited to take part in therapy (Russell et al., 2022). At the same time, it is crucial that efforts to broaden participation do not compromise the emerging therapeutic alliance with those who initially sought help, in this case Maria and Anders.

During the phone call the therapist made to plan the first session, the couple explained that they wished to attend on their own initially. Maria told the therapist that they wanted to include the children later in therapy, as their reason for returning also concerned them. The therapist sensed that

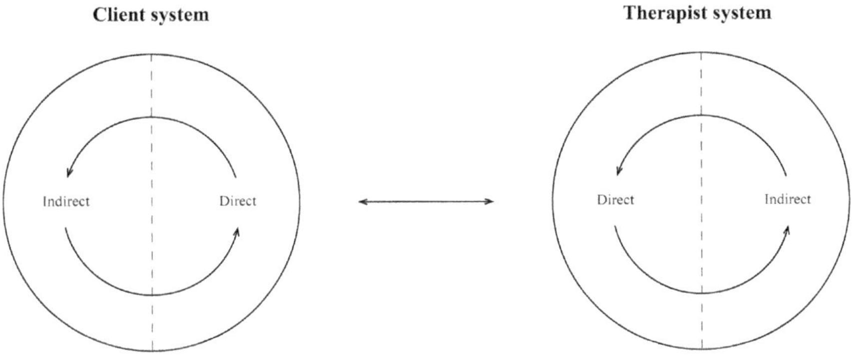

Figure 7.1 The Therapy System. From Integrative Problem-Centered Therapy: A Synthesis of Family, Individual, and Biological Therapies (p. 6), by W.M. Pinsof, 1995, New York, NY: Basic Books. Copyright 1995 by Basic Books, an Imprint of Perseus Books, LLC, a Subsidiary of Hachette Book Group, Inc. Adapted and Redrawn

Maria was withholding information, noting that she deflected the therapist's question about why they preferred not to include the children from the outset. Aware that the alliance was still in its early stages, the therapist chose not to press further. She reasoned that the parents' concerns were likely sensitive and that they preferred to share more in person.

In IST, this stance is captured by the alliance priority guideline, which holds that the therapist's primary task is to establish and maintain a satisfactory alliance with the primary clients, insofar as this serves the therapeutic process. With the initial direct client system now defined, the therapist prepared to welcome the couple to their first session together after nearly a decade.

Following this initial contact, the therapist developed a working hypothesis that the couple was seeking professional help related to parenting. This assumption was informed by her previous work with Maria and Anders, which suggested that their relationship was relatively solid, as well as by their expressed wish to include their children later in therapy. A less likely alternative hypothesis was that the parents were separating and sought counseling to help them end their relationship on good terms. The therapist chose to hold this alternative hypothesis in mind while provisionally orienting her expectations toward parenting-related concerns.

Although the therapist held some preliminary assumptions about why Maria and Anders were returning to therapy, she remained flexible, as any integrative systemic therapist would. Guided by the blueprint, she expected that new information might require her to revise or discard her working hypotheses if they no longer fit the emerging picture. The therapist had always been analytically inclined, while also being emotionally attuned to others. IST's encouragement to approach therapy as a form of inquiry, where the therapist formulates, tests, and revises hypotheses about clients' difficulties, suited her well (Pinsof et al., 2018).

The therapist often planned to meet with parents on their own before including children in therapy, although this was not a fixed rule. Decisions about whether children joined early or later were guided by the nature of the presenting problem, that is, the reason clients sought therapy and what they hoped to resolve or improve. In the case of Maria and Anders, it made sense for them to attend on their own initially. The couple had been relatively withholding about their reasons for returning to therapy, and the therapist trusted that there was a reason for this.

The following week, Maria and Anders arrived for their appointment. The first thing the therapist noticed was that Maria was visibly pregnant. She congratulated the couple on the upcoming baby, but both responded with awkward, slightly muted smiles. It was a small moment, but the therapist registered it as meaningful feedback. The working hypothesis the therapist had formed after the phone call now seemed incomplete, and she began to consider an alternative. Perhaps the couple had received troubling information about the pregnancy.

As an integrative systemic therapist, she reminded herself that her assumptions were provisional and subject to revision. She had to remain open to how the situation would take shape. Still, if something was indeed wrong with the pregnancy, she anticipated that this would likely take center stage in the conversation that followed. At this point, the hypothesizing metaframeworks the therapist held in mind were primarily development, biology, and mind (Pinsof et al., 2018). Given what the therapist could recall about the parents' religious background, she also acknowledged that the spirituality and culture metaframeworks might become relevant for understanding the case as it unfolded.

In the following conversation, the couple told the therapist that they were expecting a child with Down syndrome. The therapist spent time validating their concerns and mixed emotions, an approach intended to soothe the couple while also laying the groundwork for a strong working alliance. She focused on creating an emotional bond built on mutual trust and respect, while also beginning to understand the couple's presenting problem and how it might be resolved. The therapist knew that not only was her alliance with both Maria and Anders of great importance but equally important was the alliance they had with each other. She also considered how much Maria and Anders trusted and respected one another, whether they agreed on what had brought them to therapy, and how they each envisioned a solution.

After the session, the therapist reviewed her clinical notes and reflected on the conversation with Maria and Anders. She formed the assessment that a strong working alliance had already been established and that the relationship between Maria and Anders appeared stable. Like many integrative systemic therapists, she routinely used session-by-session systematic feedback to monitor both therapeutic progress and the quality of alliances (Tilden & Whittaker, 2022). The feedback questionnaires the couple completed at the beginning and end of the session further supported her working hypothesis: the couple's relationship appeared stable, and both the alliance between the partners and their alliance with her were strong.

At the same time, the therapist remained attentive to potential risk factors and organized these using the hypothesizing metaframeworks (Pinsof et al., 2018). The conversation had revealed that Maria had experienced postpartum depression in the period after giving birth to Jon. The therapist contemplated that a history of depression increased the likelihood of future episodes, making the mind, biology, and development metaframeworks particularly relevant. This was true both at the individual level (i.e., the mother's personal and historical vulnerability to depression) and at the family level (i.e., how taxing transitional phases in the family life cycle might trigger depressive symptoms). In addition, the parents shared concerns regarding earlier sibling rivalry between Jon and Gia. The therapist considered the possibility that Jon might respond with jealousy toward the new baby. This concern was informed by the development and mind metaframeworks, particularly in relation to family expansion, shared parental attention, and their potential impact on the sibling subsystem.

Based on her clinical experience, the therapist was not worried about how the children would respond to their baby brother's diagnosis. In families where children were given age-appropriate information and their questions were met with openness, she had yet to encounter a case in which they did not adapt. At times, this process required additional support, and the therapist was more than willing to offer this to the Peterson family.

Including the children

The following week, the entire Peterson family arrived at the therapist's office. She greeted them warmly and showed them into the therapy room. In preparation, the therapist had arranged a range of tools she found helpful when working with children: plush toys, fidget spinners, and a collection of odd rubber creatures that could be stretched and squished. The therapist had also set out her flip chart, along with colorful markers, papers, and crayons, which she laid out on the table.

The therapist was keenly aware of her responsibility to ensure that the children's experience of therapy was a positive one. She prioritized this above making the session feel productive for the parents. While this stance was partly in service of building an alliance with Jon and Gia for the purposes of the current therapy, it also reflected the therapist's broader systemic commitment to fostering positive expectations about seeking help among children.

Initially, the therapist spent time getting to know each of the children, asking about their favorite activities, their home, their friends, and other family members. When it felt natural and in service of strengthening the alliance, the therapist also shared small, age-appropriate details about herself. In time, the following exchange unfolded:

Therapist: "I know it can feel a bit strange to come to a place like this and talk to someone you don't really know, but I'm really glad you both came today! I'm curious, what did Mom and Dad tell you about why you're here?"

Gia, being the eldest, naturally took the lead.

Gia: "Well, Mom and Dad told us that our baby brother might need some extra help when he arrives, because he's going to be a little bit different."

Therapist: "Okay. And how do you feel about that, Gia?"

Gia: "I don't know. I guess that's okay. He's a baby anyway, so he's just going to cry for the bottle."

Therapist: "You're right, he's probably going to cry for the bottle, poop, and be all cute and baby-like."

Gia looked up at the therapist and giggled, while Jon remained absorbed in coloring his drawing.

Therapist: "Wow, look at what your brother has been drawing, Gia!" she said, setting up a spontaneous enactment between the siblings.

Jon: "It's us! The family!" he replied with a grin.

Therapist: "Yes, I can see that," she said, tuning in to Jon's excitement.

Jon pointed at the picture and added,

Jon: "And that's baby Tom-tom!"

Gia giggled.

Therapist: "Tom-tom?"

Jon: "Tom-tom. That's what it feels like when I touch Mommy's big belly!" he repeated enthusiastically. "TOM-TOM!"

He began patting his stomach like a drum.

Gia laughed loudly, and the rest of the family joined in.

Therapist: "That sounds like a great name," she said, reinforcing her connection with the children. She continued, "It sounds like you're both quite excited about Tom-tom arriving?"

Gia: "Yes, very much!"

Both children looked up at the therapist, beaming with delight. Although the therapist was generally cautious about posing direct questions to children, she found that carefully framed open questions could be useful when gently testing her working hypotheses.

Therapist: "Gia, what do you think will become different when baby Tom-tom arrives?"

Gia: "Sure, lots of things will be different," she said, smiling at her mother.

Therapist: "Is there anything that might feel a bit more difficult?"

Gia looked around the room, thinking. Wanting to be mindful of Jon's age while still inviting his perspective, the therapist decided to reformulate her inquiry into a circular question.

Therapist: "What do you think it might be like for Jon?" she asked, directing the question to Gia.

Gia: "Could be," she replied.

With the sibling rivalry hypothesis in mind, the therapist drew upon her knowledge of emotionally focused therapy to test it through an empathic conjecture.

Therapist: "I might be wrong, but could it be hard for him to share all that attention from Mom and Dad with a cute little baby?"

The therapist glanced empathically back and forth between the siblings.

Gia reflected for a moment while watching Jon color his drawing.

Gia: "Yeah, probably. He's a bit of a mommy's boy," she said teasingly.

Jon looked up at Gia and stuck out his tongue.

Therapist: "That makes a lot of sense, Jon," she said warmly. "When you're used to getting lots of Mom's attention, it can be hard to share it with a new baby." She continued, drawing briefly on her own experience. "It was the same with my kids. What really helped was making sure they still got some special one-on-one time, not just with me, but with their dad too. Going on little outings or having one parent read a story and snuggle up together."

Jon looked up at the therapist, appearing reassured. Feeling attuned to Jon's emotional state, the therapist offered a validating response.

Therapist: "That sounds pretty good, right?"

The therapist met Jon's gaze; they smiled at one another.

Sensing that the conversation had reached a meaningful point, the therapist decided to begin rounding off the session. She summarized what had been discussed and checked in with each family member to see whether they had anything to add. In addition to inviting verbal feedback, she handed out age-appropriate feedback questionnaires so that each family member could evaluate the session individually.

The therapist reviewed each questionnaire promptly, paying particular attention to the children's responses, once again aligning her practice with Integrative Systemic Therapy's (IST) evidence-informed guideline (Pinsof et al., 2018). The child versions of the questionnaires used a range of emojis, from frowning to smiling faces. Both Gia and Jon had selected smiling emojis.

Pointing at Jon and Gia's questionnaires, the therapist commented.

Therapist: "It seems like you guys enjoyed coming here today?"
Both Gia and Jon nodded in confirmation.

Therapist: "Maybe all of you would like to come back once more?"
Maria: "We would like that very much, wouldn't we, kids?"
Both children chimed in,
Gia and Jon: "Yes!"

The therapist and the parents continued to plan the next session. Although the baby was due in just a few weeks, they agreed to schedule a session before the due date. As always, the therapist reminded the family that they could contact her to reschedule if necessary.

After walking the Petersons out, the therapist returned to her office to write her journal note. In her assessment of the session, she noted that she was not concerned about how the children would receive their baby brother in the near future. However, the risk factors discussed with the parents in the first session, postpartum depression and potential sibling rivalry, remained present and would require continued attention.

Concluding remarks

In this chapter, we have followed the Peterson family through two initial sessions with their integrative systemic therapist. Consistent with the first step of the essence diagram of Integrative Systemic Therapy (IST), these sessions focused on convening the direct client system, defining the presenting problem, and establishing a working alliance between the therapist and the family system.

Guided by the IST guidelines, the therapist formulated working hypotheses about the family's challenges and tested them through planned interventions enacted in therapeutic conversations. Feedback from these conversations, both verbal and written, enabled her to refine and adjust her hypotheses over time. This iterative process of hypothesis formulation, intervention, and feedback is visualized in the blueprint.

In IST, a presenting problem is not treated as a fixed diagnosis or a static issue, but rather as part of an unfolding problem sequence: a patterned interaction or intrapersonal cycle that maintains or escalates distress within the family system. Families may present with multiple problems; however, in collaboration with the therapist, they agree on which problem to prioritize. By progressing through the steps of the essence diagram, the family may later shift focus to another presenting problem, continue therapy, or return to therapy at a later point to address additional concerns.

Once a prioritized presenting problem has been agreed upon, the next step in the essence diagram is to *locate the problem in a problem sequence.* The therapist then collaborates with the client system to *identify and implement a solution sequence.* The solution sequence typically introduces new perspectives, interactions, or emotion-regulation strategies that interrupt or shift the problematic cycle (Pinsof et al., 2018).

In the Peterson family, the presenting problem centered on the parents' anxiety about the baby's diagnosis. They were also worried about how having a child with potential special needs might affect the family's existing needs and dynamics. More specifically, the problem sequence involved uncertainty about how to talk with the children about these concerns, an issue further compounded by earlier experiences of postpartum depression and sibling rivalry.

As the work progressed through the steps of the essence diagram, the therapist and the family co-constructed a solution sequence through therapeutic planning. This included involving the children in a supportive context and normalizing upcoming changes in developmentally appropriate ways. Through the therapeutic conversation, the parents' worries were reframed, the children's potential concerns were explored and validated, and alternative ways of interacting following the baby's birth were discussed. Although challenges were anticipated in the near future, the family system appeared more flexible and resilient at the end of the session, as assessed by the therapist and supported by the family members' completion of systematic feedback questionnaires.

Self-reflection task

1. How do you typically begin therapy?
2. After an initial session such as the one described in this chapter, how do you usually plan for the following session?
3. Are there any clinical choices the therapist made that you would have approached differently?

References

Breunlin, D. C., & Jacobsen, E. (2014). Putting the family back into family therapy. *Family Process*, *53*(3), 462–475. https://doi.org/10.1111/famp.12083

Pinsof, W. M., Breunlin, D. C., Russell, W. P., Lebow, J. L., Rampage, C., & Chambers, A. L. (2018). *Integrative systemic therapy: Metaframeworks for problem solving with individuals, couples, and families*. American Psychological Association. https://doi.org/10.1037/0000055-000

Russell, W. P., Breunlin, D. C., & Sahebi, B. (2022). *Integrative systemic therapy in practice: A clinician's handbook*. Routledge.

Tilden, T., & Whittaker, K. J. (2022). Using ROM in family therapy. *Journal of Clinical Psychology*, *78*(10), 1973–1985. https://doi.org/10.1002/jclp.23398

Chapter 8

Case Formulation and the Process of Gathering Information

In this chapter, we introduce and demonstrate how case formulation may be used in the context of Integrative Systemic Therapy (IST). When working with children and adolescents, case formulation holds a particularly central role, as such work often entails the collection of information from multiple sources and the involvement of people beyond the close family. Case formulation thus serves as a useful tool for compiling and organizing this information (Manassis, 2014). Rather than functioning as a static document, it is understood in IST as a dynamic and evolving process that helps map the child or adolescent's systemic context, identifying patterns, interdependencies, resources, and constraints.

Formulations may be brief and provisional, appearing only as working hypotheses in the therapist's mind or recorded in the client's clinical file. They can also be more elaborate, incorporating information from multiple informants, summaries of family and extended network strengths and constraints, as well as children's drawings, genograms, feedback reports, and descriptions of important interactional sequences (McGoldrick, 2016; Pinsof et al., 2018; Tilden & Whittaker, 2022).

To guide the case formulation, the integrative systemic therapist applies central tools such as the blueprint, the hypothesis and planning matrix, and the web of human experience. By attending to the IST guidelines, the therapist keeps the case formulation problem-focused, resource-attuned, and interpersonal. Just as the implementation of treatment strategies preferably begins in the here-and-now, so too should the development of a case formulation. As the understanding of problems and relational sequences deepens, the formulation should mirror this growth, gradually integrating more of the client's history and developmental story. As therapy progresses, the formulation is continuously revised to reflect the evolving client system.

Just as treatment and assessment in IST are understood as inseparable phases of therapy, case formulation is not a one-time assessment but an ongoing process. Case formulation is a continuous dialogue with the family and its extended system, allowing the therapist and the client

DOI: 10.4324/9781003645337-10

system to co-construct a shared understanding of the problem. This collaborative process promotes engagement, ownership, and sustained focus throughout therapy. A strong case formulation supports the development of working hypotheses that guide intervention sequences and therapeutic decision-making. This is especially important when working with children and adolescents, where effective therapy often requires collaboration with broader systems. Accordingly, schools, day cares, and family members beyond the immediate family may need to be involved when gathering information necessary to inform and implement therapeutic strategies.

Although all the conceptual tools of IST lend themselves to the process of case formulation, two are particularly central when drafting a formulation: the blueprint and the web of human experience. The blueprint helps the therapist identify key resources and constraints relevant to the presenting problem, while the web of human experience provides a multisystemic overview of where such resources and constraints may be located and how they interact across systems (Pinsof et al., 2018; Russell et al., 2022).

To illustrate case formulation, we follow a therapist as she develops a working formulation based on her initial meetings with the Peterson family, introduced in Chapter 7. The Petersons are a White, Lutheran, middle-class family living just outside Decorah, a small town in northeastern Iowa. The parents are Maria (42) and Anders (47), and they have two children, Jon (5) and Gia (8). They are expecting their third child, affectionately referred to as Tom-tom. Prenatal diagnostic testing has confirmed that Tom-tom will be born with Down syndrome.

Case formulation: the Petersons

Going over her notes and reflecting on her meeting with the Peterson family, the therapist began to jot down her thoughts and impressions, organizing them under headings drawn from the web of human experience. She structured the case formulation under the heading *The Peterson Family* and created subsections for each relevant system and subsystem, including the parental and couple subsystems, the sibling subsystem, and each individual family member, as well as "Tom-tom," the baby yet to be born. Under each system and subsystem, she listed brief bullet points describing relevant theoretical perspectives and how these might hypothetically relate to the family's presenting problem. This initial step in articulating the case formulation was guided by the Integrative Systemic Therapy (IST) problem-focused guideline.

As an integrative systemic therapist, however, she was not only attentive to the problem. Guided by the strength guideline, she made similar bullet points for each subsystem's strengths and resources. Just as she had done when exploring the family's presenting problem, she wrote brief descriptions of how these resources might contribute to solving the problem, reducing constraints, or mitigating some of their negative effects. As she worked, the therapist also drew a visual representation of the family system, adding arrows between subsystems and hypothesizing how they might influence one another and the family system as a whole, and vice versa (Figure 8.1). These assumed patterns of influence were informed by the IST causality pillar, which holds that subsystems and systems influence one another, though not necessarily to the same degree (Pinsof et al., 2018). To visualize unequal influence, the therapist varied the size of the arrows; the larger the arrow, the stronger the assumed influence.

Although she could have added several more tentative arrows to describe systemic influences within the family, the therapist deliberately limited the number. She only added those she could presently relate directly to the presenting problem, in accordance with the problem-focused guideline. She then organized her working hypotheses into a table (Figure 8.2), listing how the family's resources and constraints were assumed to relate to problem maintenance or problem resolution. This overview helped the therapist maintain a balanced perspective, attending to both vulnerabilities and strengths, and guided her in choosing interventions that reduced constraints while amplifying resources. As a starting point, the therapist was satisfied with this tentative case formulation. The way she had organized the information helped her keep track of factors that might contribute either to maintaining the family's difficulties or to solving them. She also knew that new information could easily be added as therapy progressed. Although the case formulation initially appeared neat and orderly, she knew from experience that her notes would gradually become more complex and less tidy, and she was comfortable with that. For her, the formulation functioned as working notes intended to support clinical thinking in the face of family complexity, rather than as a tool for evaluating her own therapeutic successes or failures.

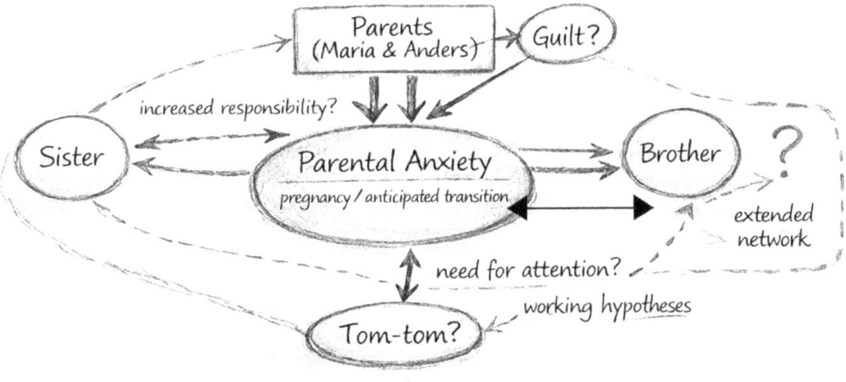

Figure 8.1 The Peterson Family: A Systemic Map of Hypothesized Influences

Subsystem	Constraints	Resources
Parental subsystem	Maria's history of postpartum depression; parental anxiety about raising a child with special needs; difficulty communicating openly with children about challenges	Willingness to seek help; reflective capacity; openness to guidance; strong motivation to support children
Couple subsystem	Potential strain from increased caregiving demands; stress may exacerbate conflicts or reduce emotional availability	Commitment to shared parenting; history of overcoming difficulties together
Sibling subsystem (Gia and Jon)	Risk of feeling overlooked due to parental focus on the new baby's needs; possible worry or confusion if not kept informed	Expressed excitement and curiosity about their baby brother; potential to be sources of joy and connection in the family
Baby ("Tom-Tom")	Anticipated medical and developmental needs associated with Down syndrome may require extensive parental resources	N/A (resources to be developed through parental and systemic support)
Extended family/ system	Uncertainty about available support and of risk isolation if broader networks are not engaged	Possibility of support from relatives, schools, and community services; cultural values of resilience and connectedness

Figure 8.2 A Systemic Overview of the Peterson Family: How to Tell the Children

As can be seen in Figure 8.2, the therapist adopted a clear systemic perspective when assessing factors related to the family's presenting problem, emphasizing relationships and interactional patterns between family members rather than focusing solely on diagnoses and symptoms of ill health. Although she was a clinical psychologist trained in the use of diagnostic manuals, she appreciated how IST offered an alternative and complementary lens for understanding the challenges faced by the families she met in practice. IST encouraged her to attend to how family adversities were expressed and sustained through relational sequences, and how such sequences could contribute to the maintenance or escalation of individual family members' mental distress.

In the case of the Peterson family, the parents entered the first session concerned about how having a third child with special needs might affect the family. More specifically, the presenting problem was how to communicate this information to their children. The parents' anxiety was further intensified by Maria's history of postpartum depression. From her perspective as an integrative systemic therapist, the parental subsystem appeared constrained by anxiety, which limited the parents' ability to initiate conversations with their children about the current situation. Drawing on the web of human experience, this constraint was assumed to be located at the dyadic (i.e., the parental subsystem) level and conceptualized within the mind metaframework. More specifically, the therapist drew on cognitive and emotional theory to hypothesize how earlier experiences contributed to negative expectations about the future, thereby maintaining anxiety-provoking communication sequences related to the pregnancy (Beck, 1976; Beck & Haigh, 2014).

Because the therapist's formulation highlighted the parents' anxiety as a central constraint on the family system, she deliberately focused her initial interventions on reducing this pressure. Already in the first session, by receiving the couple with warmth, validating their anxieties, normalizing their experience, and offering an alternative to having to tell the children on their own, the therapist facilitated a shift. The constraint of anxiety appeared to be reduced, and between sessions the parents themselves told the children that the baby they were expecting was going to be born with Down syndrome.

By the second session, when the whole family attended, they all appeared more at ease with the situation, and Gia and Jon were looking forward to meeting their baby brother. The therapist could trace this shift back to the working hypotheses articulated in her case formulation, which helped her plan a solution sequence that both acknowledged the parents' fears and facilitated more open communication within the family.

Third session

Upon reviewing her case formulation, the therapist realized that information about the family's extended network was limited. The therapist and the Peterson family had scheduled one additional session before the baby was due, and early in the third session the therapist explained her intention to learn more about the family's broader network. The family and particularly the children were eager to participate. The therapist invited them to help map out "who was who" in their network, emphasizing the value of developing a shared overview as they prepared for the arrival of the baby. This collaborative mapping would also allow the therapist to assess whether it might be helpful to invite members of the extended network into the therapy room at a later stage.

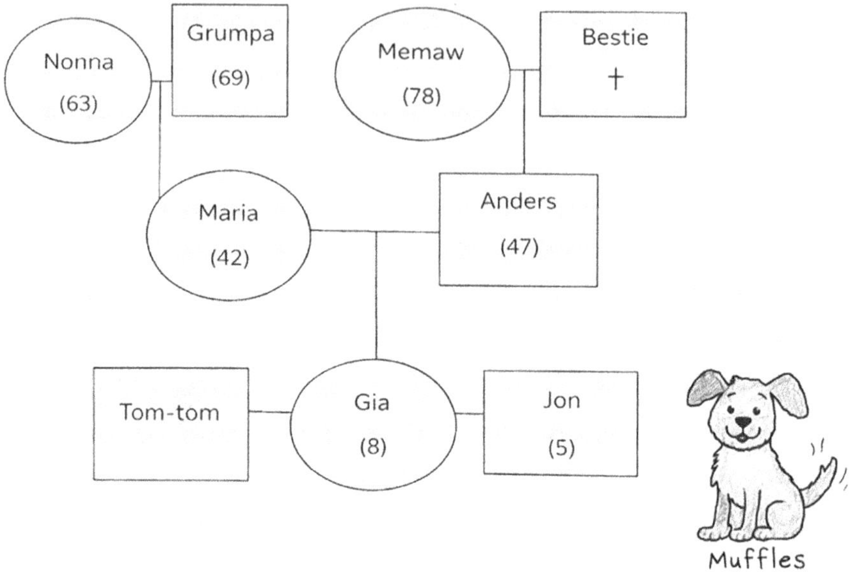

Figure 8.3 The Peterson Family Genogram

As a tool in this process, the therapist drew upon the genogram (McGoldrick, 2016) from the planning metaframework. The genogram originates from approaches associated with the past-oriented metaframeworks of the hypothesis and planning matrix, typically used when working with constraints related to family-of-origin experiences. However, the therapist also found it useful as a way of getting to know families and their extended network more fully. She had extensive positive experience using the genogram both as a component of case formulation and explicitly as intervention. In Integrative Systemic Therapy (IST), there is no distinction between assessment and intervention, as articulated in the guideline that assessment and intervention are inseparable (Pinsof et al., 2018).

In her application of the genogram, the therapist highlighted relationships between family members and their extended network, making notes of the interaction sequences including family routines and those of each family member, and how they unfolded across time. In this session, the therapist was especially attentive to Gia and Jon. She engaged them with the flip chart, inviting them to suggest who should be added to the genogram. She asked them about family members and other important relationships, letting them draw in animals, toys, or other symbols, as well as make corrections if she got something wrong. The parents were given a more observing role but contributed additions when appropriate. Toward the end of a playful yet focused session, the following overview of the family's network had appeared (Figure 8.3).

Therapist: "Wow, that's a lot of people who care about you!"

Jon: "I love my family!"

Gia: "And friends!" she chimed in.

Jon: "And Muffles!" he exclaimed, pointing to the family dog he had drawn on the flip chart.

Therapist: "Yes, we must not forget Muffles!" Validating Jon's contribution, she continued, "It seems like Memaw is important to you guys," pointing to Memaw's symbol on the genogram.

Maria: "Yes. Since my family lives in Chicago, we've become quite reliant on Anders' mom to help us out, both in general and with the children."

Anders: "Yeah, she helps out a lot, but she's not a spring chicken anymore," he sighed. Sensing this emotional shift toward anxiety, the therapist decided to put her assumption to the test.

Therapist: "Does this worry you?"

Anders: "Yes. She's not just a great support for us as a family, but her help was invaluable during Maria's illness."

As the parents spoke about their worries and the constraint within the parental subsystem became more apparent, the therapist also observed a shift in the children. Up to this point, they had been present and full of vitality; however, as the parents' worry surfaced, the children's behavior changed as well. The parents appeared not to notice this shift, preoccupied by their own thoughts and feelings. The therapist, however, observed that Gia became absorbed, her gaze drifting and her eyes glazing over, while Jon began to fidget, shifting in his seat before eventually getting up.

Anders: "Jon, sit down please," he said halfheartedly, noticing that Jon had left his seat, before glancing toward the therapist with a distant look. Noting the lack of coordination among the family members in the moment, the therapist chose to take a more directive stance.

Therapist: "That's okay. He's free to move around."

Reading this feedback from the family, the therapist revised her working hypothesis, placing greater emphasis than previously on the impact of Maria's postpartum depression on the family system. Both the mind and organization metaframeworks now appeared particularly relevant to her working hypothesis. When the parents became absorbed in memories from that period, their emotional state shifted, making them less available to their children. As a result, their leadership within the family was intermittently compromised.

Faced with this relational disconnect and uncertain how to respond, the children began to display avoidant behaviors.

Although the therapist considered exploring this revised hypothesis with the family, she judged that the timing was not right. At that moment, all family members appeared absorbed in their own internal states, turning inward and away from one another. The therapist therefore made a rapid clinical decision, drawing on the action metaframework in the hypothesis and planning matrix to intervene and bring the family back into the here-and-now. Although guided by the structure of the blueprint and its guidelines, such moments often require the therapist to improvise in response to what unfolds in the room. Taking a cue from Jon's need to move, she acted.

Therapist: "Yes, movement! Great, Jon. How about we all get up and shake some of this stuffiness off?"

The therapist rose from her chair and began shaking her arms to loosen them, gently stomping her feet. The Petersons, clearly surprised by her sudden and unexpected movement, laughed. After the initial surprise wore off, they joined in.

Reading the feedback from her intervention and noticing the family's positive response, the therapist decided to take it up a notch.

Therapist: "And now we can all become loose like spaghetti!"

She shook her arms and legs, letting them flop loosely like cooked spaghetti. The children burst out laughing and eagerly joined her. After a few more seconds of movement, the therapist settled back into her chair, and the family followed suit. The family members were once again attentive, and the therapist was able to make eye contact with each of them.

Therapist: "Nice. It seems like some movement did us all some good."

The Petersons made eye contact with one another and then looked back at the therapist expectantly. The therapist oriented herself toward the parents and continued, "It seems that discussing your anxieties not only affects you, but also ripples outward, influencing Jon and Gia, much like how a pebble thrown into water creates ripples."

Maria: "Yes, when you put it that way, it makes sense. I guess we just don't notice it ourselves."

Anders nodded in agreement.

Maria: "But now that I think about it, you're not the first person to mention this. Memaw has said something similar."

Therapist: "That makes sense. Someone who is close to you and spends a lot of time with you might notice, even if it's something that happens only occasionally."

Recognizing how eventful the session had been and judging that it was a good point at which to end with the family feeling revitalized, the therapist decided not to explore this hypothesis further at the present time. Instead, she prioritized checking in with each family member using a brief feedback questionnaire to ensure that they experienced the session as meaningful and that the themes discussed had been understood. The therapist also decided that it would be wise to meet once more with the parents before Maria gave birth, so she could share and reflect on what had become an extensive case formulation. Given that Maria's and Anders' parental capacities were now at the forefront, she judged it most appropriate to explore these issues further without the children present.

The therapist noted how the session confirmed her evolving case formulation: parental anxiety constrained the parents' availability to one another and to their children, which in turn shaped the children's behavior. This observation reinforced her systemic working hypothesis and guided her planning for subsequent sessions, illustrating how case formulation in IST remains a dynamic and dialogical process that integrates assessment, intervention, and reflection.

The following sessions

Maria and Anders accepted the therapist's offer to meet once more before the birth of Tom-tom. For this session, the therapist had prepared the Peterson family's case formulation for shared review. With only minor adjustments, Maria and Anders confirmed the therapist's working hypothesis: their anxieties about a possible return of Maria's postpartum depression and the birth of a child with special needs could, at times, preoccupy them to the extent that they became less emotionally available to Gia and Jon.

As part of the solution, the therapist proposed ongoing sessions to support the parents in managing their anxieties, alongside intermittent family sessions that would later include Tom-tom. The family also agreed to invite Memaw to upcoming sessions, thereby shifting her role from part of the indirect client system to a member of the direct client system. This would allow the therapist to share her understanding of the family's challenges with someone who was already an important resource for them and who would likely remain central as the family adjusted to the arrival of the baby. Extending the circle of participants in therapy in this way is guided by Integrative Systemic Therapy's (IST) interpersonal guideline, which emphasizes involving those relational systems most relevant to solving the presenting problem.

Guided by her case formulation, the therapist recommended that the parents contact the children's teachers to keep them informed about the situation. During the session, she and the parents discussed what would be both necessary and appropriate to share with school staff, so that Gia and Jon could receive additional support should the family's circumstances become more challenging.

The session with Memaw went well. Based on the descriptions the other family members had provided, the therapist had expected her to be understanding. Memaw revealed that she had grasped more of the situation than she had previously expressed, explaining that she had not wanted to add to Maria's burden at a time when Maria was already struggling with guilt about not being more present for her children. Although Anders had kept Memaw informed about Maria's mental health, their conversations had largely focused on practical matters related to the children.

In the session, however, they were able to talk more openly about the emotional aspects of the situation and about what the future might entail. Memaw showed a deep understanding of the parents' anxieties. The therapist helped reinforce this understanding by summarizing what was said, making the interactional process explicit as it unfolded, and validating thoughts and feelings as they arose. As a result, Memaw voiced her continued commitment to the family and her intention to help care for the children when Tom-tom arrived. She reassured Maria and Anders not to worry about her health or age, explaining that being with the children made her feel happy and alive.

Hearing this, the therapist observed how the parents softened and became calmer. She then facilitated the conversation toward planning for the month ahead, including clarifying who would take responsibility for which tasks when the time came for the birth. Four months after the birth of baby Tom-tom, a follow-up session with the whole family, including Memaw, was scheduled. The purpose of the session was to evaluate the status of the presenting problem, initially articulated as: *How do we tell the children that their baby brother will be born with special needs?* and *How will this affect them?* At the time of the session, these concerns appeared to have been resolved.

The latter issue, concerning the long-term impact on the children and the family of having a family member who may require additional care, was acknowledged as something that might become more relevant again in the future. Having *assessed the outcome*, the family agreed that the most appropriate course of action was to *conclude therapy* in accordance with the final steps of the essence diagram (Figure 3.2), with an open invitation to return should the need arise.

During the four-month period since the previous session, the postpartum depression had not returned, and at the follow-up session the family seemed in high spirits. Gia and Jon proudly showed off Tom-tom. Aside from occasional frustration from Jon, the parents had not noticed the emergence of any serious sibling rivalry. They credited this, in part, to the solution sequence developed in their previous session with the therapist. The plan entailed that Memaw regularly took the children on leisure activities and also relieved the parents for short periods so they could spend time with Jon and Gia both together and separately. This quality time with their parents was something both children cherished and spoke positively about in session. The therapist let the family fill out feedback questionnaires, pointing out and affirming how the parents had made progress on dimensions related to parental functioning.

The therapist noted that the family's progress reflected the strength of an evolving case formulation. A case formulation that integrated risks, resources, and systemic supports into a living plan helped the Peterson family navigate a major life transition with resilience.

Concluding remarks

Case formulation in Integrative Systemic Therapy (IST) is not a static diagnostic exercise, but a dynamic, dialogical, and evolving process that is continuously refined through hypothesizing, planning, conversing, and feedback. Throughout the Peterson family case, we saw how the therapist continuously revised her understanding in collaboration with the family. She balanced attention to both risks and resources and involved broader systems, such as Memaw and the children's teachers. Using tools such as the blueprint, the web of human experience, and the genogram, she was able to visualize patterns of influence, highlight constraints, and identify strengths that supported resilience. Importantly, the case illustrates how working hypotheses guided clinical choices in real time, and how those choices, in turn, fed back into the evolving formulation.

This chapter demonstrates how case formulation in IST serves as both map and compass in therapy, supporting navigation through complexity while remaining open to revision as new information emerges. By containing both problems and strengths, and by inviting collaboration across systems, case formulation becomes a living process. In doing so, it not only guides intervention but also offers a shared pathway toward resilience.

Self-reflection task

1. What is your experience of writing case formulations?
2. In what ways might the web of human experience support or enrich your case formulation process?
3. Are there any choices the therapist in the case example made that you would have approached differently?

References

Beck, A. T. (1976). *Cognitive therapy and the emotional disorders*. International Universities Press.

Beck, A. T., & Haigh, E. A. P. (2014). Advances in cognitive theory and therapy: The generic cognitive model. *Annual Review of Clinical Psychology*, *10*(1), 1–24. https://doi.org/10.1146/annurev-clinpsy-032813-153734
Manassis, K. (2014). *Case formulation with children and adolescents*. Guilford Press.
McGoldrick, M. (2016). *The genogram casebook: A clinical companion to genograms: Assessment and intervention*. WW Norton & Company.
Pinsof, W. M., Breunlin, D. C., Russell, W. P., Lebow, J. L., Rampage, C., & Chambers, A. L. (2018). *Integrative systemic therapy: Metaframeworks for problem solving with individuals, couples, and families*. American Psychological Association. https://doi.org/10.1037/0000055-009
Russell, W. P., Breunlin, D. C., & Sahebi, B. (2022). *Integrative systemic therapy in practice: A clinician's handbook*. Routledge.
Tilden, T., & Whittaker, K. J. (2022). Using ROM in family therapy. *Journal of Clinical Psychology*, *78*(10), 1973–1985. https://doi.org/10.1002/jclp.23398

Chapter 9

Strategies for Locating a Problem in a Problem Sequence

Introduction

In Integrative Systemic Therapy (IST), problems are understood as problem sequences. These are patterns of interaction in which thoughts, feelings, meaning-making, and behaviors become linked across family members and contexts. Problem sequences show how difficulties are co-constructed and maintained through ongoing cycles of interaction. By locating a problem within a sequence, the therapist can move beyond linear explanations and instead recognize how challenges are embedded in relational and contextual processes.

The blueprint for therapy and the web of human experience will be used in this chapter to demonstrate how problem sequences can be identified and understood. The blueprint will show how therapists generate hypotheses, plan interventions, and integrate feedback throughout the therapeutic process. The web of human experience is used to locate problems across different levels of systems, including person, relationships (dyads and triads), family, community, society, and global context (Pinsof et al., 2018). Together, these tools illustrate how systemic analysis provides both structure and flexibility in locating a problem within the flow of family interactions.

To illustrate the therapeutic work on problem sequences in practice, the Goodfrid family will serve as a case example throughout the chapter. Living in Des Moines, Iowa, a mid-sized city in the American Midwest, Sarah and Daniel are raising two children, Ethan (13) and Maya (9), while navigating marital tension, financial stress, and their children's contrasting developmental struggles.

Understanding problem sequences in families

In Integrative Systemic Therapy (IST), problems are not understood as an individual matter. Problems are seen as problem sequences, which are repeating patterns of interaction between family members where thoughts,

DOI: 10.4324/9781003645337-11

feelings, and behaviors are linked together in ways that perpetuate the difficulty (Lorås & Whittaker, 2025). Over time, these patterns become self-reinforcing as each person's reaction serves as feedback that shapes how others respond. Those responses, in turn, circle back and influence the first person, creating a continuous cycle of interaction. In this way, the problem is not located within an individual but in the ongoing exchanges between people.

To make this idea concrete, take the example of Ethan from the Goodfrid family. At 13, Ethan often resists doing his homework. Sarah, worried about his grades and future, reminds him again and again, hoping to motivate him. Ethan, feeling pressured, becomes irritated and withdraws. Daniel, frustrated with the tension, steps in with criticism, which only increases Ethan's anger and distance. Soon, he is avoiding not only homework but also the time with his parents. The more Ethan pulls away, the more Sarah worries and Daniel criticizes. What began as a struggle over schoolwork has evolved into a recurring cycle in which everyone's reactions perpetuate and sustain the problem.

Families who come to therapy often describe their problems in simple, individual terms. They might say that one person is anxious, lazy, or depressed. At first glance, this makes sense. It is easier to point to one person and one cause. It can feel more manageable and less confusing than trying to think about a whole set of interactions. It can also reduce the sense of responsibility for other family members. IST offers a different perspective. From this point of view, struggles such as school refusal, defiance, or anxiety are rarely considered to happen in isolation. They take shape within relationships, and they are influenced by stress, family conflict, and cultural expectations. Understanding problems as sequences helps therapists move away from blame and instead look for patterns that can be addressed (Russell et al., 2023). This shift opens up new possibilities for change. The therapist can intervene at different points in the sequence, for example, by helping parents reduce controlling behaviors, disrupting problematic coalitions between family members, or working with the couple to reduce conflict that spills over into parenting practices.

The Goodfrid family illustrates this perspective. Sarah and Daniel came to therapy because their son Ethan's school performance had declined. On the surface, it seemed like Ethan's problem was a lack of motivation, distractions, or that he was struggling academically. But as the therapist listened, a broader sequence became visible. Ethan often avoided homework after evenings when his parents argued, often about money. Daniel, already under stress, criticized Ethan for being irresponsible. Sarah, worried about Ethan's well-being, stepped in to protect him. Ethan, feeling caught in the middle, withdrew further from schoolwork and family interaction. The more he pulled away, the more his father criticized him, while his mother defended him. For example, when Sarah supported Ethan, Daniel feared that Ethan would not grasp the seriousness of the situation and felt compelled to balance Sarah's support with criticism. This, in turn, led Sarah to think that she needed to step in even more protectively, which reinforced Daniel's sense that more substantial criticism was required. Their individual attempts to improve the situation thus locked them into a problem-maintaining cycle, where each parent's actions amplified the other's response rather than alleviating the difficulty. This reveals a circular, problem-maintaining pattern in which the parents' attempted solutions activate different parts of the system in ways that sustain rather than resolve the problem (Jensen & Ulleberg, 2019). As Breunlin (1999) describes in his theory of constraints, difficulties are maintained when interactional responses intended to solve a problem inadvertently reinforce the very dynamics that keep it alive. From an IST perspective, problems are embedded in ongoing relational and contextual processes (Breunlin et al., 2011; Russell & Breunlin, 2019). What the family first saw as Ethan's individual problem was actually a problem sequence that linked marital stress, parenting patterns, and Ethan's way of coping.

Challenges in working with problem sequences

Although understanding problems as sequences opens up many possibilities for systemic intervention, it also presents significant challenges for both families and therapists. These challenges arise partly from the complexity of family life itself and partly from the habits of thought that people bring when trying to explain difficulties.

The complexity of patterns

Problem sequences are rarely simple or straightforward. Families exist within patterns of interactions, where multiple relationships co-occur between parents, between parents and children, among siblings, and between the family and the broader community (Priest, 2025). Each of these relationships can contribute to the cycle that sustains a problem. Often, they overlap in ways that make it difficult to see where one sequence ends and another begins (Whittaker & Tilden, 2022).

As mentioned, families often generate simple explanations of their problems. This is because a linear and individualistic understanding is easier to comprehend, live with, and discuss (Tyskø & Lorås, 2021). Blaming a single person or seeing the problem as a personal trait can offer clarity in the face of confusion. These explanations are also reinforced by a cultural climate that has become increasingly individualistic, where individual responsibility is emphasized, and difficulties are framed as the weakness or failure of one person (Lorås, 2017). Healthcare systems often mirror this orientation, offering quick, individualized solutions to problems that are, in reality, relational and systemic (Russell et al., 2023). In such a context, it is not surprising that family members describe problems as if they reside in one individual, since the world around them continually communicates that this is the natural way to understand difficulties. When a therapist introduces the idea that everyone contributes to the pattern, some family members may feel accused or defensive (Rimehaug & Helmersberg, 1995). Others may feel overwhelmed by the suggestion that the problem is more complicated than they thought. For this reason, integrative systemic therapists must work carefully to introduce new perspectives in ways that reduce blame and increase curiosity.

In the Goodfrid family, Ethan's school struggles showed how these overlapping patterns can operate. His difficulties were connected not only to his parents' expectations but also to his relationship with his younger sister Maya. When Ethan withdrew, Maya stepped in as "the responsible one," which sometimes led to praise from Sarah. Ethan, however, experienced this as comparison and criticism. At the same time, arguments between Sarah and Daniel about money created an atmosphere of instability that Ethan absorbed. These intertwined relationships between parents and child, between siblings, and within the couple did not function separately. They reinforced one another, creating a cycle of withdrawal, protectiveness, and frustration that no one could easily break free from.

The demand on the therapist

Working with problem sequences requires highly developed therapeutic skills. It is not enough to note what's being said. The therapist must track the timing of events, the emotions expressed, and the small yet essential details of the interaction. It also involves asking systemic questions, looking for patterns in what each person does before, during, and after a problem occurs. It also consists of holding multiple layers of context in mind, such as developmental stage, cultural norms, and external stressors (Stratton et al., 2009). As He and colleagues (2023) emphasize, the integrative systemic therapist must continually weave together psychological theory, relational dynamics, and contextual awareness to grasp how a sequence operates.

Because of the complexity of this task, the therapist's stance is just as important as their technical skills. Working systemically requires ongoing self-reflection to recognize how one's own assumptions, values, and emotional responses influence the therapeutic process (Hedges, 2010). It also calls for professional humility, meaning being aware that no single perspective captures the whole reality of a family's experience (Nissen- Lie et al., 2010; Whittaker & Tilden, 2022). Therapists must remain open to correction, be willing to learn from families, and be committed to their own professional growth through ongoing supervision and education. In this way, the practice of Integrative Systemic Therapy (IST) becomes not only a method for understanding families but also a discipline of personal and professional development (Pinsof et al., 2018; Lorås & Whittaker, 2025; He et al., 2025).

Balancing complexity and clarity

One of the biggest challenges for systemic therapy is balancing the complexity of real family processes with the need for explanations that families can actually use. If the description of the problem sequence becomes too abstract or overwhelming, family members may disengage from the discussion. On the other hand, oversimplifying the problem sequence risks reproducing individualizing explanations that Integrative Systemic Therapy (IST) transcends. The therapist's task is therefore to find ways of describing the problem sequence that highlight its relational character while remaining concrete and hopeful. Thus, the aim is not to reduce complexity for its own sake, but to translate complexity into forms of understanding that support meaningful change (Russell et al., 2023).

This balancing act is not a one-time achievement, but an ongoing process throughout therapy, as the family gradually learns to see their difficulties as part of interactional patterns. In practice, this means that the therapist actively checks with the family to see if the proposed description of the problem sequence makes sense to them. The family's perspectives are essential, since their understanding determines whether the sequence feels accurate and valuable. The therapist explores with them how they interpret the pattern, what parts they recognize from their daily life, and where they may disagree with the description. Through this process, the formulation of the problem sequence becomes a co-constructed understanding rather than an external explanation imposed on the family. In IST, this collaborative approach is supported by the iterative cycle of hypothesizing, planning, conversing, and reading feedback, which ensures that the family's reactions continually refine and shape how the sequence is understood (Pinsof et al., 2018; Russell & Breunlin, 2019).

A session with the Goodfrid family illustrates this process. Sarah and Daniel described growing concern about Ethan's increasing withdrawal from school and his resistance to attending classes. Mornings had become marked by tension, arguments, and exhaustion. As is often the case, the family initially focused on what was most visible: Ethan's refusal and the escalating conflicts surrounding school attendance.

As the therapist mapped the sequence, it became clearer how Sarah's efforts to shield Ethan from stress, Daniel's frustration about missed school days, and Ethan's withdrawal reinforced one another over time. Financial strain and ongoing marital tension further intensified these patterns. By exploring what happened before, during, and after the morning conflicts, the therapist helped the family see how each person's reaction shaped what happened next. When this description was reflected back to them, Sarah recognized how quickly she stepped in to mediate, Daniel acknowledged that he often interpreted Ethan's silence as defiance, and Maya quietly added that she usually went to her room when they started arguing because it felt "too loud and scary." Through this conversation, the family began to see the sequence as something they had co-created within a broader context of stress, rather than as an individual flaw in Ethan. In IST, such reframing helps reduce blame and shame while mobilizing the family's resources toward shared goals of change and growth (Whittaker & Lorås, 2023).

Tools for locating problems in sequences

Without clear tools, systemic concepts can remain abstract, leaving families uncertain about how to apply new insights to their daily struggles. In Integrative Systemic Therapy (IST), structured tools play a central role in bridging this gap, particularly in the identification and restructuring of problem sequences. Two such tools are especially important in this work: the blueprint for therapy and the web of human experience. Both serve the same purpose: to move families away from explanations that locate the problem in a single individual and toward an understanding of how difficulties are co-created and maintained in interaction. They provide shared maps that clarify where change is possible within the sequence and strengthen the family's sense of working together toward a common goal.

Applying the blueprint: the Goodfrid family

The blueprint for therapy (Figure 3.1) (Pinsof et al., 2018), introduced in Chapter 3, is a central guide for how the integrative systemic therapist works with problem sequences across all stages of treatment. It consists of four interconnected steps: (1) hypothesizing, (2) planning, (3) conversing, and (4) feedback (Pinsof et al., 2018). Each of the components plays a specific role in helping the therapist and the family move from an initial understanding toward meaningful change. Together, these four components form a recursive cycle. Hypotheses guide planning, which in turn shapes conversations, generating feedback that refines the hypotheses. In this way, the blueprint provides a practical structure that keeps therapy responsive, systemic, and grounded in the family's lived experiences.

When Sarah first described Ethan's school refusal as "the problem," the therapist invited each family member to share what typically happens in the morning. Ethan spoke of his sense of dread and anxiety, Sarah described pressing him to get ready for school, and Daniel explained how he tries to calm the situation but often ends up feeling caught in the middle. From these accounts, the therapist formed a tentative hypothesis about a problem sequence: Ethan's avoidance triggers Sarah's pressure, which intensifies his withdrawal and creates tension between Sarah and Daniel. Rather than locating the problem solely in Ethan, the therapist identified the problem sequence itself as the central mechanism maintaining the difficulty. This hypothesis was then shared with the family and explored collaboratively, inviting their reflections on whether the sequence resonated with their experience. Building on this hypothesis, the therapist planned to help Sarah and Daniel respond in a calmer, more unified way. Sarah would be supported in expressing her concerns without escalating pressure, while Daniel would practice standing with her rather than stepping between them. The plan was deliberately flexible, intended to guide the next steps but open to revision as new information about the problem sequence emerged.

In the following conversations, the therapist put this plan into practice. Ethan's fears about school were validated, while Sarah was invited to reflect on how her pressure, though motivated by care, often felt overwhelming to her son. Daniel was encouraged to consider how his efforts to mediate, though well-intentioned, sometimes widened the distance between him and Sarah. These exchanges not only clarified the contours of the problem sequence but also strengthened the therapeutic alliance and created a shared language for change.

As the family tried out new responses at home, feedback provided further insight into how the problem sequence unfolded in everyday life. After one morning routine, in which Sarah calmly reminded Ethan, while Daniel supported her, Ethan still resisted going to school; however, the conflict between the parents was noticeably reduced. This outcome confirmed parts of the original hypothesis while pointing to the need for refinement: reducing parental conflict was helpful, but Ethan also needed direct support in coping with school-related anxiety. The therapist therefore adjusted the working hypothesis and revised the plan to include gradual exposure to school alongside continued parental collaboration.

Applying the web of human experience: the Goodfrid family

The web of human experience (Figure 3.3), also introduced in Chapter 3, is another tool for clarifying the context of problem sequences as well as identifying factors that maintain them. While the blueprint helps map immediate cycles of interaction, the web of human experience expands the focus by situating these cycles within larger developmental, relational, and contextual domains (Pinsof et al., 2018). This broader lens enables the therapist to see not only how a sequence unfolds in the moment but also where it is maintained within the family and broader systems, and what obstacles or resources shape its course.

Like Engel's (1977) biopsychosocial model and Bronfenbrenner's (2005) ecological systems theory, the web of human experience acknowledges that families live within nested systems shaped by biology, psychology, and culture. Unlike these descriptive models, the web of human experience functions as a therapeutic tool. It actively informs case formulation by linking problem sequences to specific systemic layers and clarifying where patterns are reinforced and where interventions are likely to have the most significant effect (Whittaker & Tilden, 2022). In Integrative Systemic Therapy (IST), case formulation is therefore understood as a continuous and collaborative process through which problem sequences are mapped, revised, and clarified over time.

The web of human experience provides a structured way of organizing information within the metaframeworks, linking this information to evolving hypotheses, and refining those hypotheses through conversations with clients. Feedback plays a central role in ensuring that the formulation remains relevant. When therapy stalls, the web of human experience helps identify where change is blocked in the system. The process of refining hypotheses helps the therapist map problem sequences and identify systemic strategies that promote meaningful and lasting change (Tilden & Wampold, 2017).

When the Goodfrid family sought help for Ethan's school refusal, the therapist used the web of human experience to locate the problem sequence across several domains of family life. The exploration began with the *mind* metaframework, focusing on Ethan's inner world. He described thoughts such as "I will fail anyway" and intense morning anxiety, which led him to withdraw. Sarah responded with increased pressure to get ready, while Daniel attempted to mediate, often feeling stuck in the middle. These psychological processes reinforced the cycle of avoidance, pressure, and conflict, thereby perpetuating it.

Attention then turned to the *biology* metaframework, as Ethan reported physical symptoms such as stomachaches and headaches that made mornings feel overwhelming. Sarah tended to interpret these complaints as excuses, which only increased her urgency. Ethan, on the other hand, thought they were genuine barriers to attending school. The bodily reactions themselves became part of the trigger for the daily sequence.

From the perspective of the *spirituality* metaframework, the therapist observed how parental values influenced responses. Daniel often emphasized the importance of "being true to yourself" and encouraged Ethan to follow his own pace. Sarah, in contrast, held to the belief that persistence was a moral responsibility. These differing value-based convictions deepened the divide in how the parents approached Ethan's struggle.

Looking through the lens of the *culture* metaframework, Sarah shared that she grew up in a Mexican American family that placed strong emphasis on educational achievement. She feared criticism from her relatives if Ethan failed at school, and her concerns may also reflect broader intergenerational expectations about education as a pathway to stability and success. Daniel, raised in a family with a more relaxed attitude toward academics, experienced far less such pressure. These differences contributed to parental disagreements and amplified stress within the household. The lens of the *gender* metaframework highlighted further dynamics. Sarah saw it as her role as a mother to organize Ethan's school life and enforce routines, while Daniel felt pressure to remain the calm, stabilizing presence in the household. These gendered positions became rigid, limiting the couple's ability to respond flexibly as a team.

The perspective of the *development* metaframework sheds light on Ethan's developmental needs. As an adolescent, his resistance was not only about anxiety but also about his push for autonomy. Sarah's pressing collided with his developmental need for independence, intensifying the sequence. By reframing Ethan's behavior as part of normal adolescent development, the therapist could help the family see the problem in a broader context.

Finally, the therapist considered the *organization* metaframework and how it applied to the family. Morning routines were poorly coordinated: Sarah tried to manage every detail, while Daniel stayed back until conflict erupted. This left Sarah overwhelmed, Daniel reactive, and Ethan caught in the middle. The organizational structure of daily life reinforced the very patterns the family was struggling with.

By systematically moving through the web of human experience, the therapist and family came to see Ethan's school refusal not as a single problem anchored in him, but as a problem sequence maintained by multiple overlapping factors: psychological distress, biological symptoms, parental values, gendered roles, cultural expectations, developmental transitions, and organizational routines. This broader understanding helped refine the working hypothesis and pointed toward systemic strategies for change, supporting Ethan's coping skills, restructuring daily routines, and aligning parental roles with both cultural pressures and developmental needs.

Concluding remarks

Working with problem sequences highlights the heart of systemic practice. The therapist's central task is to reveal how difficulties are sustained through circular patterns of interaction, rather than being located within a single individual. Making such patterns visible in a way that is concrete, collaborative, and hopeful can be transformative in itself. It reduces blame and shame, strengthens engagement, and creates possibilities for families to see themselves as active participants in change. Careful exploration of what happens before, during, and after a problematic event helps illuminate these dynamics and turns them into shared material for conversation.

Within this broader task, the blueprint for therapy and the web of human experience play a supportive role. The blueprint provides a step-by-step structure for hypothesizing, planning, conversing, and integrating feedback, while the web of human experience broadens the lens, ensuring that hypotheses are situated within multiple layers of human life, including mind, biology, culture, gender, organization, development, and spirituality. When used together, these tools allow the therapist to move fluidly between the practical structure of therapeutic work and the broader systemic contexts that shape family problems.

From a systemic perspective, the tools are not an end in themselves but part of a larger effort to help families recognize how their difficulties are woven into ongoing interactional sequences and to co-create opportunities for change. By holding together structure and complexity, the therapist fosters a process that honors the uniqueness of each family while maintaining a systemic orientation that supports lasting transformation.

Self-reflection task

1. When a family presents a problem as located in one individual, how can you shift the focus toward a problem sequence in a way that reduces defensiveness and invites shared responsibility?
2. How can the blueprint for therapy and the web of human experience help you formulate and communicate a problem sequence in a way that balances systemic complexity with clarity for the family?
3. How might the therapists' personal assumptions influence how problem sequences are understood and addressed in therapy?

References

Breunlin, D., Pinsof, W., & Russell, W. (2011). Integrative problem-centred metaframeworks therapy 1: Core concepts and hypothesizing. *Family Process*, *50*(3), 293–313. https://doi.org/10.1111/j.1545-5300.2011.01362.x

Breunlin, D. C. (1999). Toward a theory of constraints. *Journal of Marital and Family Therapy*, *25*(3), 365–382. https://doi.org/10.1111/j.1752-0606.1999.tb00254.x

Bronfenbrenner, U. (2005). The bioecological theory of human development. In U. Bronfenbrenner (Ed.), *Making human beings human* (pp. 3–15). SAGE Publications.

Engel, G. L. (1977). The need for a new medical model: A challenge for biomedicine. *Psychodynamic Psychiatry*, *40*(3), 377–396. https://doi.org/10.1521/pdps.2012.40.3.377

He, Y., Hardy, N., Fisher, A., & Venketramen, N. (2025). *Integrative systemic supervision: Training therapists to work with individuals, couples, and families.* Taylor & Francis.

He, Y., Hardy, N. R., Fisher, A. R., & Lokotama, I. (2023). Development of the integrative systemic therapist. *Fokus på Familien* [Focus on the family], *4*(51), 315–331. https://doi.org/10.18261/fokus.51.4.4

Hedges, F. (2010). *Reflexivity in therapeutic practice.* Bloomsbury Academic. https://doi.org/10.5040/9781350390362

Jensen, P., & Ulleberg, I. (2019). *Mellom ordene- kommunikasjon i profesjonell praksis* [Between Words—Communication in Professional Practice]. Gyldendal.

Lorås, L. (2017). *The map of competences in systemic therapy. A qualitative study of the systemic competences in Norwegian child and adolescent mental health that target the associated abnormal psychosocial situations in axis 5 (ICD-10)* [Doctoral thesis]. East London University in conjunction with the Tavistock Clinic.

Lorås, L., & Whittaker, K. J. (2025). Integrativ systemisk terapi [Integrative systemic therapy]. In L. Lorås & O. Ness (Eds.), *Håndbok i familieterapi* [Handbook in family therapy] (pp. 283–298). Fagbokforlaget.

Nissen-Lie, H. A., Monsen, J. T., & Rønnestad, M. H. (2010). Therapist predictors of early patient-rated working alliance: A multilevel approach. *Psychotherapy Research*, *20*(6), 627–646. https://doi.org/10.1080/10503307.2010.497633

Pinsof, W. M., Breunlin, D. C., Russell, W. P., Lebow, J. L., Rampage, C., & Chambers, A. L. (2018). *Integrative systemic therapy. Metaframeworks for problem solving with individuals, couples and families.* American Psychological Association. https://doi.org/10.1037/0000055-000

Priest, J. (2025). *The science of family systems theory.* Routledge.

Rimehaug, T., & Helmersberg, I. (1995). Barnepsykiatrisk utredning- Fra produkt til prosess. Veien mot rollen som med- ekspert [Child Psychiatric Assessment—From product to process. The path toward the role of co-expert]. *Fokus på Familien* [Focus on the family], *23*, 145–156.

Russell, W. P., & Breunlin, D. C. (2019). Transcending therapy models and managing complexity: Suggestions from integrative systemic therapy. *Family Process*, *3*(58), 641–655. https://doi.org/10.1111/famp.12482

Russell, W. P., Breunlin, D. C., & Lofton, H. C. (2023). Integrative systemic therapy: A feedback-driven perspective. *Fokus på Familien* [Focus on the family], *4*(51), 293–314. https://doi.org/10.18261/fokus.51.4.3

Stratton, P., Pote, H., Cottrell, D., Boston, P., Shapiro, D., & Hanks, H. (2009). *The Leeds systemic family therapy manual: Therapist adherence protocol, training edition.* Leeds, LFTRC.

Tilden, T., & Wampold, B. E. (Eds.). (2017). *Routine outcome monitoring in couple and family therapy: The empirically informed therapist.* Springer. https://doi.org/10.1007/978-3-319-50675-3

Tyskø, E. H. D., & Lorås, L. (2021, 15 September). God psykisk helse skapes gjennom våre relasjoner [Good mental health is made within our relations]. *Adresseavisen*. https://www.adressa.no/debatt/i/KzJxG7/han-er-stille-for-han-svarer-vi-er-her-for-a-forandre-pa-meg

Whittaker, K. J., & Lorås, L. (2023). Integrativ Systemisk Terapi som tilnærming i arbeid med sammensatte problemer [Integrative Systemic Therapy as a therapeutic approach to compounded problems]. *Fokus på familien* [Focus on the family], *4*(51), 332–348. https://doi.org/10.18261/fokus.51.4.5

Whittaker, K. J., & Tilden, T. (2022). Integrativ systemisk terapi: Metateori og psykoterapeutisk praksis [Integrative systemic therapy: Metatheory and psychotherapeutic practice]. *Fokus på Familien* [Focus on the family], *3*(49), 190–206. https://doi.org/10.18261/fokus.50.3.2

Chapter 10

Identifying and Implementing a Solution Sequence

Introduction

In the previous chapter, we examined how problem sequences can be identified and mapped as recurring cycles of interaction within the family system. Recognizing these cycles shifts the focus from blaming an individual to understanding difficulties as patterns sustained in relationships. Yet awareness alone is not enough. Real change requires that families reorganize their familiar patterns into what we call a solution sequence. A solution sequence is not simply the absence of conflict, but rather the emergence of new interactional patterns that resolve or improve the presenting problem and alter the sequences that maintain it.

Within Integrative Systemic Therapy (IST), this shift from problem to solution is understood as a central movement in therapy. The aim is not only to interrupt unhelpful sequences but to co-create alternative ways of relating that acknowledge each member's needs for belonging and individuality. Such changes are rarely achieved through isolated techniques or one-sided efforts. Families often return to the comfort of old patterns, even when those patterns are unhelpful. Sustainable change requires collaboration. Thus, the therapist, parents, and children all take active roles in shaping and testing new responses that can gradually stabilize into a solution sequence.

The move toward solution sequences also highlights the importance of process over quick fixes. In IST, change is not reduced to correcting behavior or removing symptoms, but involves the careful reorganization of the family's interactional patterns. When families experience themselves as co-authors of these new patterns, the solutions become both more credible and more enduring. This chapter draws on the blueprint for therapy, the web of human experience, the essence diagram, and the hypothesis and planning matrix, presented in Chapters 3 and 6, to show how solution sequences can be developed and sustained.

DOI: 10.4324/9781003645337-12

In this chapter, the Carter family will serve as a case example to illustrate how solution sequences can be identified and implemented in practice. Living in Plano, a suburban community in Texas, North America, Michael and Aisha are raising their two children, Lucas (11) and Harper (15). They are navigating increasing strain related to Harper's growing independence and Lucas's escalating sibling conflicts. Harper has recently become more withdrawn and resistant to parental involvement, while Lucas reacts to tension at home with impulsive outbursts and rivalry toward his sister. What initially appears as adolescent defiance and sibling conflict gradually reveals a more complex pattern of misattuned responses, parental uncertainty, and shifting developmental needs.

What is a solution sequence?

A solution sequence refers to the reorganization of interactional patterns so that circular, problem-focused responses are interrupted and replaced by new patterns that foster connection, regulation, and collaboration. In systemic terms, the goal is not to eliminate conflict or remove symptoms, but to shift the family's dynamics toward patterns that create space for resilience and growth.

In Integrative Systemic Therapy (IST), solution sequences emerge when the family experiments with alternative responses that interrupt established loops and generate new feedback cycles. These are rarely dramatic or immediate changes. Instead, they often begin as small, deliberate shifts in everyday interactions that gradually accumulate into a new pattern. For example, when parents adjust their responses to a child's withdrawal or escalation, their new responses alter the sequence's flow and make different outcomes possible. Over time, repeated and reinforced exchanges consolidate into a new cycle that is experienced as more supportive and less problem-maintaining (Russell & Breunlin, 2019).

The notion of a solution sequence is closely tied to IST's emphasis on process. The blueprint for therapy reminds us that change unfolds through iterative cycles of hypothesizing, planning, conversing, and integrating feedback. At each stage, the emerging solution sequence is tested, refined, and adjusted. The web of human experience situates these changes within broader contexts, ensuring that they are not only interactionally coherent but also aligned with the psychological, developmental, cultural, and organizational dimensions of family life (Whittaker & Lorås, 2023).

A brief example from the Carter family helps clarify this idea. When Harper withdrew and resisted parental involvement, Michael often responded with firmer expectations and attempts to reassert structure, while Aisha stepped in to soften the tension and protect Harper from further conflict. This created a loop of distance, correction, and escalating frustration, which Lucas frequently reacted to through impulsive outbursts or attempts to draw attention away from the tension. A solution sequence in this case did not mean eliminating disagreement about rules or independence, but supporting Michael and Aisha in coordinating new responses that reduced escalation and created space for Harper to express her need for autonomy without withdrawing from connection. This illustrates how a solution sequence emerges not as a fixed prescription but as a collaborative repatterning of interaction.

Transforming problem sequences into solution sequences

Problems are maintained through circular patterns of interaction that repeatedly limit possibilities for change (Russell et al., 2023; Pinsof et al., 2018). The principle of circularity highlights how each person's response becomes the context for the next, creating ongoing feedback loops that reinforce the very patterns the family wishes to change. Because the interactions are emotionally charged, family members can come to feel as if they are trapped in a cycle, responding in ways they do not actually want to, but feel powerless to avoid. Over time, the circular pattern creates a sense of inevitability: "This is just how we are as a family." In systemic terms, the patterns can be understood as constraints that narrow the family's repertoire of responses and channel behavior into rigid, self-reinforcing pathways (Breunlin, 1999).

In Integrative Systemic Therapy (IST), the therapist's task is not merely to interrupt problem sequences, but to facilitate the development of more adaptive interactional patterns. For example, instead of a parent escalating pressure when a child resists, the parent might pause, acknowledge the child's emotion, and invite collaboration on the next step. The child, feeling less attacked, may be more open to responding constructively. In this way, the interaction shifts from a self-reinforcing problem sequence to a more adaptive solution sequence.

A solution sequence is not a one-time fix but an ongoing process. New patterns are co-created in the family's everyday life, often starting with small experiments that elicit different responses. Over time, repeated small shifts can consolidate into relational patterns that feel both more flexible and more sustainable. The therapist supports the process by helping family members recognize moments of choice, rehearse alternative responses, and reflect on how these interactions can change the emotional climate (Whittaker & Lorås, 2023). In this sense, IST frames therapy as a process of cultivating new ways of living together, where the family experiences themselves not as stuck, but as capable of creating change.

The Carter family illustrates this process. In their problem sequence, Harper's withdrawal and resistance to parental involvement prompted Michael to increase structure and enforce expectations more firmly, while Aisha sought to soften the tension and protect Harper from escalating conflict. This dynamic heightened Harper's distance and contributed to growing frustration between the parents. Meanwhile, Lucas reacted to the tension with impulsive outbursts that further intensified the atmosphere at home. Each step of the cycle reinforced the next: Harper withdrew further, Michael became more corrective, Aisha more protective, and Lucas more reactive. The result was a well-rehearsed loop of distance, correction, triangulation, and escalating tension.

A solution sequence begins when each person makes even a minor adjustment that interrupts the established pattern. Michael, for example, might shift from immediately reinforcing rules to first acknowledging Harper's desire for independence, expressing expectations in a calmer and more attuned manner. Harper, instead of withdrawing completely, might experiment with staying in the conversation a little longer, perhaps voicing her need for space without shutting down. Aisha, rather than stepping in to buffer the tension, might support Michael openly, while still validating Harper's perspective, signaling coordination rather than division. Lucas, in turn, might receive clearer reassurance and attention outside the conflict, reducing his need to react impulsively when tension rises. None of these shifts alone resolves the broader challenges around autonomy and family tension. Yet when connected, these adjustments begin to alter the emotional climate: there is less escalation, more clarity, and a growing sense of shared direction.

The emergence of solution sequences highlights an essential principle: change is not abstract but observable and embodied in interaction. New patterns can be seen in the family's everyday language, the pacing of conversations, the way eye contact is maintained, or how parents position themselves in relation to one another and their children. In practice, the therapist helps the family notice such moments of difference, reinforcing that change is not only possible but already underway (Tilden & Wampold, 2017).

Because old patterns are deeply ingrained, transformation requires repetition. Families need opportunities to rehearse alternative responses, reflect on what felt different, and refine their approach to support their children. Here, the therapist's role is both supportive and directive, guiding the family back to small successes when stress threatens to pull them into old cycles. Over time, repetition strengthens confidence that new ways of interacting can be sustained outside the therapy room.

Equally important, the shift from problem to solution changes the meaning of the difficulty itself. When an issue is no longer attributed to a single individual but understood as part of a sequence, blame and shame diminish. Families begin to see themselves not as stuck in an identity of dysfunction, but as capable of co-creating more constructive cycles. This systemic reframing not only reduces tension but also activates the family's own resources, aligning their efforts toward a shared goal of adaptation and growth (Russell et al., 2023).

Strategies for facilitating solution sequences

Shifting from a problem sequence to a solution sequence involves more than simply replacing one behavior or relational pattern with another. It entails a reorganization of how the family coordinates emotions, attention, and action in response to stress. In Integrative Systemic Therapy (IST), this shift is built collaboratively. While solutions may emerge from multiple sources, including the clients themselves, the therapist increasingly draws on the hypothesis and planning matrix (Figure 6.1) as constraints are identified to guide treatment strategies. The child's experience is taken seriously, parental roles are clarified and supported, and the therapist provides a structure for trying out new responses and learning from the outcomes. When a family begins to experience even small moments of reduced reactivity and improved collaboration, these moments are treated as seeds of a new pattern that can be practiced, reinforced, and extended (Russell et al., 2023). In this sense, solution sequences are not merely individual adjustments but systemic openings in which previously constrained possibilities become available (Breunlin, 1999).

The blueprint for therapy keeps this work intentional. Hypotheses connect what the family hopes to change with a concrete map of the sequence that perpetuates the problem. Plans translate the hypothesis into observable next steps, such as coordinating parental responses to Harper's withdrawal or establishing clearer agreements about autonomy and responsibility. Conversations prepare the ground by building alliance, aligning expectations, and rehearsing new interactional moves. Feedback then closes the cycle, clarifying what reduced tension, what intensified it, and where further adjustments are needed (Pinsof et al., 2018; He et al., 2023). In the Carter family, this meant identifying the value of coordinated parental responses, experimenting with a new way of addressing Harper's need for independence without escalation, and refining the approach when Lucas's reactivity signaled lingering tension. The process is circular rather than linear, allowing progress to endure despite inevitable setbacks (Bertrando & Lorås, 2021; Tilden & Wampold, 2017).

The web of human experience broadens the picture, allowing the solution to have enough anchors to hold. Changes in family interaction are easier to sustain when they align with the adolescent's developmental need for increasing autonomy, consider sibling positioning, acknowledge cultural expectations about independence and responsibility, and attend to physiological factors such as sleep and emotional arousal (Pinsof et al., 2018; Whittaker & Tilden, 2022). For the Carter family, recognizing Harper's developmental push for independence, clarifying parental roles in responding to conflict, and creating predictable moments of connection that also included Lucas all supported the same aim. The solution sequence did not depend on a single adjustment but on several coordinated shifts, each reinforcing the others.

Several strategies can be particularly effective in the active work of helping families make the shift from problems to solutions:

- **In-session experiments.** The therapist may invite family members to rehearse alternative responses in real time, such as having Michael practice acknowledging Harper's need for independence before stating expectations, while Harper practices staying engaged in the conversation rather than withdrawing. Aisha might rehearse supporting Michael's message while still validating Harper's perspective, signaling coordination rather than division. These experiments are valuable because they move the family from reflection to action. They allow members to experience the impact of a new response in the moment, making change tangible rather than theoretical. Such exercises also illustrate the therapist's dual stance as both supportive and gently challenging, a position that strengthens the family's confidence in experimenting with new interactional patterns (Whittaker & Lorås, 2023).
- **Language shaping.** Therapists can introduce new words and metaphors that soften blame and highlight possibility. Instead of framing Harper as "defiant" or "withdrawn," the therapist might describe her as pushing for autonomy or disengaging when overwhelmed, shifting attention from individual fault to developmental needs and relational dynamics. For example, moments of tension might be reframed as "a negotiation about independence" rather than a power struggle. Systemic practice assumes that language is not merely descriptive but constitutive: how families talk about themselves shapes what they experience as possible (White, 2008; Tilden, 2023).
- **Structuring the conversation.** By slowing the conversation and asking each person to speak in turn, the therapist creates space for perspectives that might otherwise be overshadowed. This not only balances participation but also models a new rhythm of interaction that contrasts with the family's habitual escalation. Even brief moments of calmer conversation can be treated as significant "exceptions" to the problem cycle, and drawing attention to them helps consolidate the sense that change is already underway (Russell & Breunlin, 2019).

These strategies represent only a few ways therapists can facilitate movement from rigid problem sequences toward more adaptive solution sequences. They illustrate how integrative systemic therapists work in the space between family interaction and therapeutic intervention, drawing on the web of human experience to structure the process and ensure that broader layers are considered. Other strategies may be equally important depending on the family and the context, and many more are discussed in Chapter 6 when describing the use of the hypothesis and planning matrix. Still, the principle remains the same: solution sequences are co-constructed collaboratively or emerge when therapists help families experiment with new responses, reflect on their effects, and integrate feedback into the evolving sequences of interaction.

Implementation and continuation of the solution sequences

Implementation of a solution sequence occurs at the fourth step of the essence diagram (Figure 3.2), and it is perhaps the most fragile step in the early phase of therapy. Families often come to therapy with the hope of rapid transformation and can feel discouraged when new patterns are difficult to enact or old patterns resurface. In Integrative Systemic Therapy (IST), this is anticipated and reframed. Relapses into the problem sequence are not viewed as a failure, but rather as information (Russell et al., 2023). This perspective rests on the systemic understanding that family systems are self-regulating. When one part of the system shifts, other parts often attempt to restore balance by pulling interactions back into familiar forms (Priest, 2025). The therapist's role is to help the family analyze what happened at the moment of return to the old cycle, whether it was a missed cue, a familiar emotional trigger, or a role slipping back into place, and to use this information to refine the plan. At times, the intervention is simplified to make change more manageable. At other times, the plan is supported by practical aids such as brief parental coordination before addressing Harper, agreed-upon phrases to signal rising tension, or predictable moments of one-on-one connection with Lucas to reduce reactive competition. In the Carter family, expanding the plan to include structured yet flexible conversations about independence, alongside clearer parental alignment, became a crucial adjustment. What distinguished this phase was not the absence of setbacks, but the family's growing capacity to use moments of renewed tension as information for learning and refinement. At times, however, efforts to modify or strengthen the solution sequence do not lead to its initial or sustained enactment. In such cases, the therapist and family may collaboratively explore what might be constraining the emergence of new patterns, a focus developed further in Chapter 11.

Sustainable change also requires that families experience ownership of the solution. Enduring change is more likely when it is developed collaboratively, meaning that family members experience their voices and perspectives as shaping the strategies being tried (Whittaker & Lorås, 2025). In IST, this means that Harper's push for autonomy is taken seriously as meaningful information, that Michael and Aisha are invited to coordinate rather than critique one another, and that the therapist models humility and transparency by keeping their hypotheses open to conversation and revision (He et al., 2023). This creates a reflective space where new possibilities are not prescribed but discovered together in conversation (Lorås & Whittaker, 2026). In the Carter family, for example, Harper's articulation of her need for space became a central reference point, not as an act of defiance, but as a shared signal guiding how conversations about expectations and independence were reorganized. Such collaborative meaning-making is what makes solution sequences resilient. They are not external techniques imposed on the family, but internalized ways of responding that feel coherent and authentic to each member.

Generalization is the next step. A solution sequence that stabilizes one setting, such as the morning routine, must find pathways into other contexts if it is to endure. IST emphasizes that problem and solution sequences are not isolated events but systemic patterns that travel across situations and relationships (Pinsof et al., 2018). In practice, this means that a calmer, more coordinated response in the morning can also shape how the family approaches homework, mealtimes, or transitions at the start of the week. The therapist plays an active role in helping the family script these extensions, anticipate predictable stressors, and prepare simple repair moves if tension rises. In this way, changes are more likely to generalize beyond the therapy room and across situations. This generalization is reinforced through feedback from family members (Whittaker & Lorås, 2023). Concrete indicators, such as the number of conflict-free mornings, ratings of stress intensity, or the ability to recover after tension, provide tangible evidence of progress. Celebrating these small wins anchors hope and reinforces the sense that new family stories are being written (Whittaker & Lorås, 2025). Such symbolic recognition of progress does more than encourage; it strengthens the family's sense of identity as capable of co-creating new cycles.

Concluding remarks

Implementing a solution sequence in Integrative Systemic Therapy (IST) is a disciplined yet flexible practice. It requires more than interrupting entrenched problem patterns. The task is to create space for new relational patterns that can be rehearsed, stabilized, and eventually carried forward by the family. The blueprint for therapy keeps the process intentional by placing hypotheses, planning, conversations, and feedback in continual conversation. Within this structure, the hypothesis and planning matrix provides a focused decision-making framework, guiding the therapist in selecting interventions that align with the working hypothesis and target specific points in the interactional sequence where change is most likely to occur. The web of human experience broadens this lens, reminding the therapist that no solution sequence is sustainable unless it resonates with the family's developmental stage, embodied experience, cultural meanings, values, and organizational context. Feedback then informs the therapist about how the family is responding, whether adjustments are needed, or whether the new pattern is gaining stability.

At its core, the process underscores that families change through interaction rather than instruction. Collaborative engagement protects dignity and distributes responsibility in ways that reduce blame and enhance agency. When family members experience themselves as co-creators of the new sequence, change becomes less fragile because it is woven into everyday life rather than dependent on the presence of the therapist. In this sense, implementing solution sequences is not only about resolving an immediate difficulty but also about strengthening the family's systemic capacity for resilience.

Self-reflection task

1. When working to transform a problem sequence into a solution sequence, how can you ensure that the new interactional pattern is developed collaboratively with the family rather than introduced as a therapist-driven correction?
2. How can the hypothesis and planning matrix guide your decisions when identifying and implementing a solution sequence within the family's interactional patterns?
3. When a family returns to an old problem sequence, how can you adopt a failure-driven stance that treats setbacks as information for strengthening the solution sequence?

References

Bertrando, P., & Lorås, L. (2021). Systemisk- dialogisk individualterapi [Systemic- dialogical individual therapy]. In P.-E Binder, L. Lorås, & F. Thuen (Eds.), *Håndbok i individualterapi* [Handbook in individual therapy] (pp. 307–318). Fagbokforlaget.

Breunlin, D. C. (1999). Toward a theory of constraints. *Journal of Marital and Family Therapy*, *25*(3), 365–382. https://doi.org/10.1111/j.1752-0606.1999.tb00254.x

He, Y., Hardy, N. R., Fisher, A. R., & Lokotama, I. (2023). Development of the integrative systemic therapist. *Fokus på Familien* [Focus on the family], *4*(51), 315–331. https://doi.org/10.18261/fokus.51.4.4

Lorås, L., & Whittaker, K. J. (2026). Integrative systemic therapy. In O. Smoliak, E. Tseliou, T. Strong, S. Bava, & P. Muntigl (Eds.), *The Routledge international handbook of postmodern therapies* (pp. 249–262). Routledge.

Pinsof, W. M., Breunlin, D. C., Russell, W. P., Lebow, J. L., Rampage, C., & Chambers, A. L. (2018). *Integrative systemic therapy. Metaframeworks for problem solving with individuals, couples and families.* American Psychological Association. https://doi.org/10.1037/0000055-000

Priest, J. (2025). *The science of family systems theory.* Routledge.

Russell, W. P., & Breunlin, D. C. (2019). Transcending therapy models and managing complexity: Suggestions from integrative systemic therapy. *Family Process*, *3*(58), 641–655. https://doi.org/10.1111/famp.12482

Russell, W. P., Breunlin, D. C., & Lofton, H. C. (2023). Integrative systemic therapy: A feedback-driven perspective. *Fokus på Familien* [Focus on the family], *4*(51), 293–314. https://doi.org/10.18261/fokus.51.4.3

Tilden, T. (2023). Hvilken nytte har vi av modell? [What use do we have for models?]. *Fokus på Familien* [Focus on the family], *4*(51), 270–292. https://doi.org/10.18261/fokus.51.4.2

Tilden, T., & Wampold, B. E. (Eds.). (2017). *Routine outcome monitoring in couple and family therapy: The empirically informed therapist.* Springer. https://doi.org/10.1007/978-3-319-50675-3

White, M. (2008). *Maps of narrative practice.* W.W Norton & Company Inc.

Whittaker, K. J., & Lorås, L. (2023). Integrativ Systemisk Terapi som tilnærming i arbeid med sammensatte problemer [Integrative Systemic Therapy as a therapeutic approach to compounded problems]. *Fokus på familien* [Focus on the family], *4*(51), 332–348. https://doi.org/10.18261/fokus.51.4.5

Whittaker, K. J., & Lorås, L. (2025). Integrativ systemisk terapi [Integrative systemic therapy]. In L. Lorås & O. Ness (Eds.), *Håndbok i familieterapi* [Handbook in family therapy] (pp. 283–298). Fagbokforlaget.

Whittaker, K. J., & Tilden, T. (2022). Integrativ systemisk terapi: Metateori og psykoterapeutisk praksis [Integrative systemic therapy: Metatheory and psychotherapeutic practice]. *Fokus på Familien* [Focus on the family], *3*(49), 190–206. https://doi.org/10.18261/fokus.50.3.2

Chapter 11

Identifying and Addressing Constraints

Introduction

As discussed in the previous chapter, developing a solution sequence is an essential step in therapy. Yet sustaining change is rarely straightforward. Even when families begin to establish more constructive interactional patterns, progress can be disrupted by conditions that limit their ability to maintain these changes. In Integrative Systemic Therapy (IST), such conditions are described as constraints. A constraint is not simply resistance or a lack of effort, but any systemic factor, whether psychological, relational, biological, cultural, or organizational, that reduces the family's ability to enact and sustain new ways of relating (Breunlin, 1999).

In IST, constraints are seen as natural outcomes of adaptive processes. Families constantly balance the dynamics of belonging, individuality, and responses to stress. When this balance is unsettled, constraints manifest as rigid or repetitive patterns that maintain the system's stability (Priest & Lorås, 2026). Thus, the therapist's task is not to impose external solutions, but to help the family notice these patterns and strengthen their ability to reorganize interactions in more flexible and supportive ways. IST offers a metaframework for this work. The blueprint for therapy structures hypotheses and interventions so that therapeutic efforts remain focused and purposeful. Within this structure, the web of human experience provides a template for understanding factors that may constrain family process and problem resolution. The web of human experience broadens this perspective by integrating the hypothesizing metaframeworks, *development*, *biology*, *culture*, *mind*, *gender*, *spirituality*, and *organization*, across multiple levels of the family and its extended system. The hypothesis and planning matrix guides clinical decision-making by providing options for intervention that target the constraints that have been identified in a manner consistent with IST's planning guidelines. Systematic feedback, understood as both structured and creatively adapted methods for eliciting clients'

DOI: 10.4324/9781003645337-13

perspectives, provides additional guidance for identifying where change becomes constrained and for adjusting the process so that solution sequences can be re-established and maintained.

Focusing on constraints highlights a crucial dimension of IST. It is often through addressing these limitations that families develop the flexibility needed for sustainable change. This chapter, therefore, examines the role that constraints have in therapeutic practice.

The Berg family will serve as a case example. Camilla and Henrik live in the small town of Steinkjer in the Trøndelag region of mid-Norway, where they are raising their children, Elias (14) and Ida (8). They are navigating ongoing couple difficulties that repeatedly pull the family into cycles of tension. These conflicts not only strain the parental relationship but also affect Elias and Ida, who respond with withdrawal and somatic complaints, respectively, further constraining the family's ability to sustain new patterns of interaction.

Constraints as a core concept in Integrative Systemic Therapy

Constraints refer to psychological, relational, biological, cultural, or contextual conditions that limit a family's capacity to initiate or sustain new solutions (Breunlin, 1999). They are not signs of failure but predictable features of complex systems striving to maintain equilibrium. Rather than reducing them to individual resistance, Integrative Systemic Therapy (IST) understands constraints as systemic factors that keep families from instituting new patterns and adaptations, even when motivation for change is strong (Priest, 2025). These may include factors such as illness or past trauma; feelings of isolation or bullying at school; generational differences within families; or policies that restrict access to childcare or healthcare. Any factor within the web of human experience may potentially act as a constraint, limiting the implementation of solution sequences.

Constraints operate across multiple levels of family life and are expressed through ongoing patterns of interaction within the family and its broader context. Within the web of human experience, different dimensions interact and reinforce one another, shaping how constraints are maintained over time. Mapping these interactions helps identify where flexibility is restricted and where focused intervention is needed to support change.

Constraints often become most visible when families struggle to enact or maintain emerging solution sequences. In these moments, constraints can be understood as part of how the family attempts to preserve stability. Families continually negotiate belonging and individuality while responding to perceived or real threats (Priest & Lorås, 2026). When this balance becomes strained, interactional patterns may become more rigid, reducing flexibility and making it harder to sustain new ways of relating. The therapist's task is therefore to identify where regulation falters, to develop hypotheses about the function these patterns serve, and to collaborate with the family to reduce their constraining effects. In this way, constraints guide intervention by pointing to where new interactional possibilities need to be strengthened.

The Berg family illustrates how constraints can operate in practice. Initially, Camilla and Henrik sought couple therapy for recurring conflicts in their relationship. Through therapy, the couple began to establish a solution sequence in which conflicts were de-escalated, allowing for clearer articulation of emotions. Efforts were also made to implement a strategy to shield the children from tension if it were to rise. For a period, this created greater calm in the home. Yet the progress proved fragile.

Long-standing patterns of criticism and withdrawal resurfaced under stress, especially in moments involving everyday decisions about routines, responsibilities, and expectations for the children. Instead of presenting a coordinated and predictable joint leadership, Camilla and Henrik slipped back into polarized positions. These tensions unsettled the family climate and directly affected Ida, who responded with withdrawal and recurring stomach pain, particularly before school. Elias, in turn, distanced himself from family interactions and increasingly spent more time alone, reducing opportunities for repair and connection. From an IST perspective, these developments were understood as indicators of deeper systemic constraints affecting both the organization of the family system and the well-being of its members. Unresolved relational patterns between the parents limited the family's capacity to stabilize the emerging solution sequence. The system was embedded in a web of influences that included Camilla's strong reactions to uncertainty, Henrik's tendency to disengage when conflict arose, Elias's withdrawal from family interactions, and Ida's somatic responses to parental strain. To address these constraints, including unresolved emotional wounds in the couple relationship, the therapeutic focus temporarily shifted back toward strengthening the couple relationship as a foundation for stabilizing change in the family system.

What followed was a consolidation of the parental alliance, which was a prerequisite for restoring emotional safety for the children and maintaining new interactional patterns in everyday life. In line with Pinsof and colleagues' (2018) description of the blueprint for therapy, the therapist moved from hypotheses to targeted planning. The hypothesis and planning matrix guided the selection of interventions, which included emotionally focused conversations that enabled Camilla and Henrik to articulate underlying fears and needs. The work also involved psychoeducation on stress regulation and developmentally sensitive conversations with the children in family sessions. Ongoing systematic feedback was used to monitor shifts in the family climate and to detect early signs of renewed constraint. By framing the situation as a web of interconnected constraints across family and broader systems, the therapy remained consistent with family systems theory and opened space for more flexible and sustainable change (Pinsof et al., 2018; Priest, 2025; Priest & Lorås, 2026).

Understanding constraints conceptually becomes meaningful when they are recognized in interaction. They may appear in subtle shifts in tone, recurring misunderstandings, or lack of emotional regulation. At the same time, integrative systemic therapists must attend to how constraints may arise from factors beyond immediate interaction, such as individual vulnerabilities, contextual stressors, or broader cultural and environmental influences. These factors, in turn, shape the family's relational patterns. Constraints are therefore identified not merely through what families report, but through observations of how interaction between family members unfolds in the room, how such patterns are sustained over time, and how these patterns may be shaped by influences across multiple levels of the system. Constraints often become particularly visible when families struggle to enact or maintain emerging solution sequences. The following section outlines how therapists can systematically identify constraints by attending to interactional sequences, communicative cues, and the ongoing systematic use of feedback.

Identifying constraints in practice

In therapy, constraints often become visible through patterns of communication. They are not always immediately observable but emerge through tone of voice, timing, pauses, or shifts in emotional intensity when sensitive topics are raised.

Communication theory distinguishes between a content level and a relational level (Watzlawick et al., 1967). What is said conveys content, while how it is said expresses the quality of the relationship and the emotional context. Although constraints are often reflected at the relational level, they may also appear in the content itself, for example, through recurring themes, rigid or problem-saturated narratives, or accounts that reflect limited access to resources or experiences of discrimination.

When therapists ask family members what prevents them from enacting a solution sequence, the content of their responses can reveal intrapsychic, interactional, historical, or contextual constraints that need to be addressed. The interaction between content and relational levels may also indicate underlying constraints, such as when what is said does not align with the emotional tone, giving rise to ambiguity or misunderstandings (Christiansen, 2023).

In session, therapists recognize constraints by paying attention to both what is communicated and how it is communicated, such as subtle shifts in tone of voice and body posture. Such cues can reveal tension even when the words themselves appear collaborative. Reactions that may appear to be resistance or avoidance may, from a systemic perspective, actually represent attempts to protect relationships or maintain stability. The therapist's task is to see these moments as part of ongoing communicative patterns rather than isolated incidents.

Constraints often manifest as mismatches, minor discrepancies between stated intentions and actual behavior, or as differences in how family members describe difficulties or progress. These discrepancies can also appear when improvement in one area is quickly offset by tension in another. In communication theory terms, such processes reflect feedback loops that regulate interaction, sometimes reinforcing unhelpful patterns rather than supporting change (Christiansen, 2023).

In Integrative Systemic Therapy (IST), observing feedback loops provides insight into how the system is organized. When Camilla and Henrik once again slipped into familiar patterns of criticism and withdrawal, this was not interpreted as evidence of therapeutic failure, but rather as a sign that deeper relational constraints were limiting their progress. Similarly, Elias's increasing distance and Ida's stomach pain were understood as expressions of stress within the system. This stance makes curiosity possible instead of disappointment and helps the family recognize that communication itself is the vehicle for both maintaining and transforming patterns.

Systematic feedback is one of the most effective ways to identify constraints. As described in Chapter 12, systematic feedback may include both structured instruments and developmentally adapted methods that provide regular insight into symptoms, relational quality, alliance, and overall well-being. When such feedback is reviewed collaboratively, differences in perspective often become visible and can open new lines of inquiry. The therapist might ask what stands out most in the feedback or how it feels to notice that family members experience progress differently.

Families are often surprised when they see their answers side by side, and this can open up new conversations about differences in perception. In the Berg family, the feedback revealed that while Camilla and Henrik experienced periods of improved communication, both children continued to report distress linked to tension at home. Elias described withdrawing to avoid conflict, and Ida reported stomach pain on days when arguments escalated. When the family reviewed their responses together, it became clear that the children were more affected by the parental strain than the parents had recognized. What had seemed like relational improvement proved to be uneven and vulnerable to renewed conflict. The feedback highlighted that ongoing tension and relational misattunement continued to constrain the family's ability to stabilize new interactional patterns.

The blueprint for therapy supports this work by providing a flexible structure that enables the therapist to move seamlessly between hypotheses, planning, conversations, and feedback (Pinsof et al., 2018). The blueprint functions as a responsive map that evolves in tandem with the family's understanding. In practice, the therapist might reflect aloud and invite exploration through questions such as,

> What else could be influencing what happens when tension rises at home? Could old patterns between Camilla and Henrik be re-emerging under stress? How might Elias's withdrawal or Ida's stomach pain be connected to the atmosphere between you? And how are external pressures from work or daily responsibilities adding strain?

Framing the discussion in this way helps the family see therapy as an adaptive and collaborative process. Obstacles are understood as signals that the system is under pressure and attempting to restore balance.

During evaluation of the therapy (see the essence diagram, Figure 3.2), working with the blueprint clarified that the family's difficulty was not primarily about isolated conflicts, but about how recurring tension in Camilla and Henrik's relationship shaped the emotional climate of the home. The reflection led to minor but meaningful adjustments, such as brief parental check-ins before discussing sensitive topics, clearer agreements about how to handle disagreements in front of the children, and more conscious attention to emotional tone during stressful moments. These adjustments helped stabilize everyday interactions and reintroduced a sense of predictability, making further progress possible.

Creative use of the web of human experience in session may help make such systemic processes visible. Drawing on this conceptual tool, therapists can collaborate with the family to create a visual representation of interactional dynamics, identifying relevant dimensions across the family and extended system that influence one another. During such an externalizing exercise, family members are invited to contribute their own observations about what increases stress and what promotes stability. For the Berg family, the resulting map included Camilla's heightened fear of losing control in conflict, Henrik's tendency to withdraw in an effort to reduce further conflict, Elias's distancing in response to parental strain, and Ida's somatic complaints when arguments intensified. Seeing these interconnected circular patterns helped the family understand that the difficulties did not reside within one individual but within the interactional system linking them together. This shift from blame to shared understanding strengthened collaboration and opened space for more sustainable change.

Addressing constraints in therapy

Addressing constraints is not only a technical task but also a relational one. How they are introduced and discussed depends on the quality of the alliance between the therapist and the family. A strong alliance makes it possible to approach constraints with openness rather than defensiveness. The therapist's approach, including tone, timing, and curiosity, helps the family experience the conversation as collaborative and respectful rather than critical (Tilden & Vrabel, 2021). When therapists frame constraints as part of the family's adaptive effort instead of as personal shortcomings, they communicate respect and validate the family's competence. The meaning of a constraint is therefore co-constructed through conversation, where the therapist's language can either reinforce defensiveness or open new ways of understanding. When communication conveys safety, curiosity, and equality, families are more willing to explore what keeps them constrained.

In the Berg family, the most pressing constraint was the recurring tension between Camilla and Henrik. Their disagreements about responsibility, communication, and emotional expression spilled into everyday life and weakened their ability to provide a stable and predictable environment for the children. To address this, the therapist consulted the hypothesis and planning matrix and decided to shift the therapeutic focus. This involved adding more focused couple sessions alongside the regular family meetings. The intensified couple work, in parallel with whole-family sessions, aimed to strengthen the parental alliance so that the system as a whole could stabilize.

During the couple sessions, Camilla and Henrik were encouraged to articulate underlying expectations, fears, and coping strategies. At one point, Camilla said, "When conflicts escalate, I feel I have to take control. Otherwise, everything falls apart." Henrik responded, "When things get intense, I withdraw because I'm afraid of making it worse." These exchanges revealed how their interactional pattern reinforced tension rather than regulation.

To keep changes small and testable, the therapist introduced a weekly review process guided by the Integrative Systemic Therapy (IST) blueprint (Pinsof et al., 2018; Breunlin et al., 2011). The blueprint organized the next steps in a concrete and collaborative way. The therapist suggested, "Let us choose one small adjustment, try it for a week, and then reflect together on what happened and whether it needs refining." Based on the hypothesis that parental misalignment heightened the children's stress, the weekly plan focused on three elements: first, brief parental coordination before discussing sensitive topics; second, a shared pause if conflict escalated; and third, an explicit statement of a shared parental intention before re-engaging. The following session reviewed what worked and what required adjustment. This structure made the process predictable and adaptive rather than corrective. Within this weekly cycle, systematic feedback supported fine-tuning. Feedback conversations helped illuminate subtle shifts in family climate, including Ida's somatic responses when tension rose and Elias's distancing when conflicts intensified. Rather than being viewed as individual problems, these reactions were treated as indicators of systemic strain.

In short, addressing constraints in IST involves reducing patterns that sustain tension while strengthening processes that support regulation and collaboration. For the Berg family, this meant integrating couple and family sessions, making systematic use of feedback, drawing on interventions selected through the hypothesis and planning matrix, and revisiting both the blueprint and the web of human experience to maintain alignment. A simple repair agreement was also established: if conflicts escalated repeatedly over a short period, the parents would pause, use their agreed repair steps, and revisit their shared intentions before re-engaging. Gradually, these practices reduced the constraints and allowed the emerging solution sequence to stabilize.

Concluding remarks

Working with constraints is a defining aspect of Integrative Systemic Therapy (IST). Constraints reveal how family systems regulate themselves and where change encounters resistance. When these constraints are acknowledged and addressed, the family's ability to sustain solution sequences increases. This focus keeps therapy coherent and systemic, as it invites therapists to explore the relational and contextual conditions that shape behavior rather than searching for individual faults.

Grounded in family systems theory, IST understands every family as an interdependent and self-regulating system (von Bertalanffy, 1969; Priest & Lorås, 2026). Constraints often emerge when this self-regulation becomes rigid, and the system's efforts to maintain balance inadvertently limit its ability to adapt. From this perspective, internal feedback loops can constrain the system's ongoing attempts to adapt. The therapist's role is therefore not to impose change, but to help the family restore its capacity for balanced interaction, where belonging, individuality, and emotional regulation coexist in a dynamic equilibrium. This systemic stance keeps the therapeutic focus on interactional processes rather than isolated systems, emphasizing how each member's response both shapes and is shaped by the others.

Through the web of human experience, IST approaches constraints from a flexible, multisystemic perspective. Constraints are identified via observation, conversation, and systematic feedback, and are addressed through collaborative interventions guided by the blueprint. The hypothesis and planning matrix helps turn systemic hypotheses into focused, observable adjustments across system levels, ensuring that interventions remain aligned with identified constraints. This perspective positions the therapist not as an expert who removes obstacles, but as a facilitator who helps families notice, understand, and gradually shift the forces that constrain them.

Importantly, constraints are not viewed as failures, but as valuable information about where the system's resources are not yet fully accessible. When therapy slows down or progress stalls, these moments signal that existing constraints are limiting the family's ability to draw on strengths, capacities, and relational supports already present. Seen in this way, "failures" become opportunities to identify what restricts flexibility and to mobilize resources that have been obscured by tension or misalignment. Each small, deliberate adjustment, whether in communication, emotional coordination, or daily routines, can reopen access to these resources and create new pathways for growth and increased flexibility.

By treating constraints as integral to the systemic process of change, IST equips therapists to remain curious, responsive, and hopeful. Addressing constraints invites a deeper exploration of how family members communicate, regulate, and adapt to one another. It transforms therapy from a process of merely correcting problems to one of restoring movement and vitality within the system. In this sense, constraints are not obstacles to overcome but openings through which meaningful and sustainable change can emerge.

Self-reflection task

1. How do you distinguish between resistance and systemic constraints in therapy?
2. How can the blueprint, the web of human experience, the hypothesis and planning matrix, and feedback help you identify and address constraints hindering progress?
3. How might constraints represent adaptive attempts to preserve stability or belonging within the family?

References

Breunlin, D., Pinsof, W., & Russel, W. (2011). Integrative problem-centred metaframeworks therapy 1: Core concepts and hypothesizing. *Family Process*, *50*(3), 293–313. https://doi.org/10.1111/j.1545-5300.2011.01362.x

Breunlin, D. C. (1999). Toward a theory of constraints. *Journal of Marital and Family Therapy*, *25*(3), 365–382. https://doi.org/10.1111/j.1752-0606.1999.tb00254.x

Christiansen, J. C. V. (2023). Fem grunnleggende antagelser om kommunikasjon [Five basic assumptions about communication]. In F. Thuen & L. Lorås

(Eds.), *Lærebok i kommunikasjon* [Textbook in communication] (pp. 44–60). Fagbokforlaget.

Pinsof, W. M., Breunlin, D. C., Russell, W. P., Lebow, J. L., Rampage, C., & Chambers, A. L. (2018). *Integrative systemic therapy. Metaframeworks for problem solving with individuals, couples and families.* American Psychological Association. https://doi.org/10.1037/0000055-000

Priest, J. (2025). *The science of family systems theory.* Routledge. https://doi.org/10.4324/9781003491972

Priest, J., & Lorås, L. (2026). *Familiesystemteori. Teori, evidens og praksis* [Family systems theory. Theory, evidence and practice]. Fagbokforlaget.

Tilden, T., & Vrabel, K. A. (2021). Fellesfaktorer i psykoterapi [Common factors in psychotherapy]. In P.-E. Binder, L. Lorås, & F. Thuen (Eds.), *Håndbok i individualterapi* [Handbook in individual therapy] (pp. 89–104). Fagbokforlaget.

von Bertalanffy, L. (1969). *General system theory: Foundations, development, applications.* George Braziller.

Watzlawick, P., Bavelas, J. B., & Jackson, D. D. (1967). *Pragmatics of human communication.* Norton.

Chapter 12

Use of Feedback Tools in Family Therapy with Children and Adolescents

Introduction

Feedback may be understood as the fuel that moves the therapeutic process forward. It is the continuous stream of information that therapists rely on, moment by moment, to evaluate whether their current approach is working and to make informed decisions about what to do next. Within Integrative Systemic Therapy (IST), feedback is incorporated as one of the four core components (hypothesizing, planning, and conversing) of the blueprint. Through feedback, therapists and clients collaboratively assess whether adaptive solutions are taking hold or whether the therapeutic process is constrained, thereby signaling the need to update working hypotheses and adjust treatment strategies.

Continually seeking feedback from clients is the most reliable way to determine whether they experience the therapeutic process as meaningful and valuable. In the course of therapy, assessments of clients' progress are often based primarily on the therapist's own judgment. However, such assessments can be problematic, as research has demonstrated severe limitations in therapists' intuition and observational accuracy (Hannan et al., 2004). As a result, clinicians do not always recognize treatment failure or deterioration as it is occurring (Lambert et al., 2003). The use of feedback tools in psychotherapy helps counteract these limitations by providing therapists with ongoing, client-generated information concerning their progress in treatment.

Importantly, systematic feedback tools may also reduce social desirability and conformity pressures that can arise when clients are asked directly by the therapist how therapy is going. In such situations, clients may offer positive feedback despite experiencing limited benefit. Systematic feedback enables clients to communicate their experience of progress or lack thereof, in a way that feels less confrontational, while still influencing the direction of therapy. In this way, feedback tools facilitate communication not only between therapist and client but also among family members attending therapy. From this perspective, systematic feedback can be understood as

DOI: 10.4324/9781003645337-14

one of the most important strategies a therapist may make use of to ensure genuine user involvement, giving clients voice and influence and thereby strengthening collaboration (Tilden & Wampold, 2017).

A substantial body of research supports the positive impact of feedback-informed treatment with adults (e.g., Barkham et al., 2023). Although fewer studies have been conducted with children and adolescents, the existing evidence is promising, though not yet conclusive, regarding the effects of feedback on treatment outcomes in these populations (Bergman et al., 2018; Chiauzzi, 2021). Taken together, these findings support the broader argument for building and sustaining therapeutic cultures in which feedback, whether gathered systematically through questionnaires or by other means within sessions, is actively valued and integrated into clinical practice.

IST is a therapeutic approach that has fully embraced the added benefits of routine feedback, a commitment reflected not only in the blueprint but also in the IST guidelines. For example, routine use of feedback directly supports the problem-focused principle of IST and aligns with the guideline stating that assessment and intervention are inseparable processes. The systematic gathering of client feedback also represents an empirically informed and cost-effective practice (Barkham et al., 2023).

Feedback systems

Although some feedback systems assess a wide range of outcomes and processes, it is generally recommended to use instruments that require minimal time for clients to complete and are easy for therapists to score and interpret (Barkham et al., 2023). Within Integrative Systemic Therapy (IST), therapists are encouraged to incorporate formal feedback instruments as part of routine clinical practice, while adapting their use to the needs of the client system. Many advanced digital platforms for delivering and evaluating structured feedback are available. However, these are often costly and can be challenging to use in public-sector settings due to data protection requirements.

While digital versions of feedback questionnaires offer clear advantages, such as ease of delivery, completion, scoring, evaluation, and archiving, paper-and-pencil versions allow for greater flexibility and creativity. For example, clients may add notes or comments, provide multiple ratings to reflect different time points or contexts, or use drawings and other visual elements to communicate their experience. Although such additions are not always easily quantifiable, this flexible use of feedback is clinically meaningful. It is particularly valuable when working with children and adolescents who may feel constrained, overwhelmed, or otherwise unable to engage with questionnaires when they are used in a more rigid manner.

This highlights an important principle: within IST, feedback tools should not be understood solely as assessment tools, but perhaps even more importantly as conversational tools intended to promote change. Accordingly, the primary purpose of feedback is not to generate data, but to facilitate dialogue and reflection and to strengthen collaboration throughout the therapeutic process. Before examining how various forms of structured feedback may be used as conversational tools, we will first outline a selection of useful systems for delivering and reporting such feedback. These examples are intended to illustrate possibilities within feedback-informed practice and are not meant to limit the use of other systemic feedback instruments.

Systemic therapy inventory of change

The systemic therapy inventory of change (STIC; Pinsof et al., 2015) is an integrative and comprehensive feedback system developed specifically for use within Integrative Systemic Therapy (IST). It comprises multiple components assessing therapeutic outcomes and processes, as well as relevant demographic information. Consistent with IST principles, the STIC emphasizes not only clients' difficulties but also the resources available within the client system. The system allows parents to provide information about themselves, their partner, their children, and the family as a whole across six domains of the web of human experience. Following a more extensive initial assessment, the STIC is designed to collect session-by-session feedback that informs real-time clinical decision-making throughout the course of therapy (Pinsof et al., 2018).

The STIC is a psychometrically sound instrument, and recent research has shown that IST supported by the STIC yields better treatment outcomes than IST conducted without it (Pinsof et al., 2024). Although the system was intentionally designed to minimize client burden, it remains more time-consuming to complete than the other systems featured in this chapter.

Partners for change outcome management system

The partners for change outcome management system (PCOMS; Duncan et al., 2003a; Miller et al., 2003) is a brief, user-friendly feedback system designed to support feedback-informed treatment across therapeutic modalities. In contrast to more extensive progress-monitoring systems, PCOMS consists of two ultra-brief visual analogue scales: the outcome rating scale (ORS), typically completed at the beginning of each session, and the session rating scale (SRS), completed at the end of the session. Together, these measures provide a rapid snapshot of client functioning and well-being, as well as an assessment of the quality of the therapeutic alliance.

In contrast to the STIC, PCOMS is not designed with family systems theory in mind. Because all items are posed at the individual level, the system offers limited information about the broader relational systems of which clients are a part, making it less informative in complex family therapy cases. Nevertheless, PCOMS has strong psychometric properties (Anker et al., 2009). Its accessibility and brevity have contributed to its widespread use across a range of public-sector settings.

A notable feature of PCOMS is its adaptation for use with children from the age of 6. Like the adult versions, the child outcome rating scale (CORS; Duncan et al., 2006) and the child session rating scale (CSRS; Duncan et al., 2003b) are brief visual analogue scales. However, rather than using text-based anchors, the child versions employ emojis, with a sad face anchoring the left side and a happy face anchoring the right side of each scale. The domains assessed in the CORS and CSRS mirror those of the adult versions but use simpler language: "me," "family," "school," and "everything" for the CORS, and "listening," "how important," "what we did," and "overall" for the CSRS.

Although PCOMS for children and adolescents has not yet been extensively researched, studies conducted in school counseling contexts have yielded promising results (Cooper et al., 2013, 2019). Taken together, these features make PCOMS a practical option when therapists require a brief, easy-to-administer feedback tool that can be flexibly integrated into conversations with both children and adults, particularly in settings where time and resources are limited.

The marriage and family therapy practice research network

The marriage and family therapy practice research network (MFT-PRN; Johnson et al., 2017, 2025) is a digital platform developed by researchers and clinicians at Brigham Young University. It includes an array of brief, transtheoretical instruments for routine monitoring, as well as more comprehensive measures assessing client demographics and background characteristics. Similar to PCOMS, many of these instruments use visual analogue scales for scoring and assessment.

Beyond assessing family functioning, the platform is highly flexible and can be configured to monitor different relational subsystems across treatment, for example, the alliance between the therapist and each family member, as well as alliances among family members themselves (Anderson et al., 2024). Many of the questionnaires are suitable for adolescents to complete. This flexibility, combined with the digital format that enables ongoing tracking of progress on presenting problems, makes the MFT-PRN particularly well suited for use within Integrative Systemic Therapy (IST), especially in outpatient settings where assessment needs to be both brief and clinically meaningful. The instruments available within the platform have demonstrated satisfactory psychometric properties (e.g., Anderson et al., 2021, 2024).

The dialogical feedback tool

The dialogical feedback tool (DFT; Rober et al., 2020) is an easy-to-use, qualitative, two-item questionnaire designed specifically for work with young children who have basic writing skills or who can be supported in completing the form. Each of the two questions is accompanied by a character, one disgruntled and the other happy. Each character has a speech bubble in which the client can write what the character would say about the session. The same question is posed for both characters: *What would he say about the session?* In this way, the DFT prompts the clients, from young children to adults, to express both positive and negative feedback about the session. The DFT is not designed to track outcomes over the course of therapy, but rather to function as a conversational tool that supports the establishment and maintenance of the therapeutic alliance. Due to its qualitative nature, it does not lend itself to psychometric evaluation.

In summary, the feedback systems presented in this chapter vary in their level of extensiveness, the degree to which they assess family functioning, and their suitability for younger clients. Comprehensive systems such as the STIC offer rich, multisystemic information that explicitly supports the hypothesizing and planning metaframeworks of Integrative Systemic Therapy (IST), while more flexible digital platforms, such as the MFT-PRN, allow therapists to tailor feedback monitoring to the needs of specific client systems and treatment contexts. PCOMS, with its ultra-brief questionnaires, facilitates rapid alliance and outcome monitoring in busy clinical settings, whereas qualitative tools such as the DFT are particularly well suited for work with young children in contexts where monitoring outcomes over time is not essential. Regardless of which feedback system is used, the common denominator from an IST perspective is that feedback is understood not primarily as data gathering, but as a means of sustaining dialogue, collaboration, and therapeutic responsiveness (Tilden & Whittaker, 2022).

Creativity and feedback

The systematic use of feedback does not necessarily need to take the form of a questionnaire. When working with children, it is often advantageous to use alternative formats such as drawing, illustration, and play. A variety of tools have been developed for this purpose, including board games (e.g., *Hei: the feelings and situations game*; Mindme, 2021) and different types of systemic representation figures and conversation cards designed for children. Although many such tools are commercially available, they may also be handmade by a creative therapist or co-created with the child or adolescent during the session.

For example, in our work with divorced families, we often invite the child to draw the two homes in which they live. If a child appears hesitant, we may begin by asking curious, concrete questions about their homes and, if needed, sketch simple elements ourselves. In our experience, children usually engage quickly and often take over the drawing once the process is underway. Sessions of this kind are frequently initiated at the request of a parent who feels they lack a sufficiently clear understanding of how their child experiences life across two households. Communication between parents may be limited, and each parent often holds different impressions of how the child is functioning in their respective homes. Directly asking the child how they feel about living in two homes rarely yields elaborate responses; more often, such questions evoke visible discomfort or distress.

Gathering feedback from children about their lived experience therefore needs to be nonconfrontational, curiosity-driven, and grounded in a systemic perspective. This includes offering children opportunities to talk about friends, family members, pets, and leisure activities, all contextualized within their broader social world. Using a flip chart or other large sheet of paper, together with colored crayons, can greatly support this process. The act of drawing family and social networks, including important places, routines, and relationships, helps externalize and organize the child's experiences. This not only assists the child and therapist in making sense of the child's relational world but also provides parents with valuable insight into the child's perspective, resources, and competencies. Such drawings typically unfold over several sessions and may be revisited throughout therapy, either to add new elements or to return to aspects of the picture that become relevant as the therapeutic process evolves.

Working creatively with different tools to facilitate conversations and evoke feedback from children and adolescents can be both meaningful and rewarding for everyone involved. Meeting children and adolescents where they are developmentally, with curiosity, understanding, and creativity, strengthens the therapeutic alliance not only between the child and therapist but also among the family members attending the sessions. Such approaches enable children to communicate their inner experiences through both verbal and nonverbal means, thereby enriching the therapeutic dialogue and strengthening systemic connection.

When working with children who are too young, otherwise unable to answer questions themselves, or who do not attend sessions on a regular basis, it may be useful to invite parents to complete questionnaires on the child's behalf. The child outcome rating scale (CORS; Duncan et al., 2006) lends itself well to such use with only minor adaptations. In these situations, parents are asked to complete the questionnaire instead of the child, using instructions such as: *How do you think your child would score on these four dimensions?*

These dimensions refer to the child's overall well-being, the child's experience of how things are in the family, the child's experience of how things are going at school, and the child's overall experience when all aspects of life are taken into consideration. Importantly, such ratings should be understood as reflections of parental perspectives rather than direct representations of the child's experience and are best used as starting points for dialogue rather than as definitive assessments.

When both parents are present, this approach also creates an opportunity to compare their responses regarding how the child is faring. Divergent ratings often provide a valuable starting point for constructive conversations about similarities and differences in parental perspectives, parental collaboration, and what each parent might do differently to facilitate positive change for their child. When used in this way, parent-reported feedback becomes a relational and dialogical resource that supports shared understanding and collaborative problem-solving.

In some instances, it is not possible or appropriate to use questionnaires or other structured feedback tools. In such situations, feedback may instead be gathered verbally at the end of the session. McLeod (2017) has suggested systematically inviting clients to reflect on moments of particular value following each session, for example, by asking: *Was there a moment during the session that was of special value to you?* From an Integrative Systemic Therapy (IST) perspective, this question is particularly useful because it anchors feedback in concrete moments of action, emotion, and meaning-making, rather than in abstract evaluations of the session as a whole.

Research on common factors in psychotherapy has shown that corrective emotional experiences play a central role in bringing about meaningful therapeutic change (e.g., Whiting et al., 2025). By explicitly inviting clients to identify moments of particular value, such feedback questions draw attention to these experiences and may support their integration within the therapeutic process. In this way, verbal feedback not only informs the therapist's ongoing hypothesizing and planning but may also deepen clients' awareness of change as it is occurring.

In our own practice, we have further adapted this question by reformulating it in a circular manner, for example, *Mum, was there a moment during this therapy session that you perceived as being of special value for your son?* Our experience is that such questions, by placing family members in a mentalizing position, serve not only an assessment function but may also be therapeutic in their own right. They foster curiosity about one another's inner experiences and relational perspectives and represent valuable alternatives when other feedback tools are unavailable, such as in online sessions or when time constraints limit the use of standardized measures.

Feedback in practice

In this section, we present a series of clinical vignettes illustrating situations that may arise when systematic feedback is used in therapy. While the first example demonstrates how therapists may introduce and explain the rationale for using systematic feedback in family therapy, the subsequent vignettes move beyond instances in which progress is simply validated. Instead, they address common and clinically important challenges, such as lack of progress, divergent feedback among family members, and alliance ruptures. Through these examples, we illustrate how feedback in Integrative Systemic Therapy (IST) functions not merely as information, but as a catalyst for reflection, dialogue, and therapeutic action.

Presenting the rationale

Presenting the rationale for using systematic feedback is perhaps the most important step in implementing feedback-informed practice. If therapists do not succeed in conveying the purpose and value of feedback questionnaires, clients are less likely to engage meaningfully with them or to complete them consistently. In the following vignette, we illustrate how a therapist introduces the use of systematic feedback in family therapy.

Therapist: I have a set of questionnaires that I use in my work.

(The therapist lays the questionnaires out on the table so everyone can see them.)

I ask clients to fill these out every session. The reason I use them is that they help me understand what each of you, and the family as a whole, might need help with. It's a bit like taking your temperature each time we meet. It gives me important information so I can better understand what's going on and how to be most helpful to you. Does that make sense?

(The therapist briefly explains the questionnaires.)

Do you have any questions so far?

(The therapist answers questions and elaborates as needed.)

And just to be clear, if at any point you don't feel like filling these out, please let me know. If any questions come up while you're completing them, I'd really like you to tell me.

(The family completes the questionnaires.)

Thank you all for filling these out. I really appreciate it. Would it be okay if we place them together and talk about what stands out or catches your attention?

(If a family member prefers not to share, the therapist offers to look at the questionnaire privately and follow up accordingly.)

In this vignette, we demonstrate one way of presenting systematic feedback in therapy. There is no single correct way of doing this; however, it is essential that therapists clearly explain how the feedback will be used. For clinical purposes, it is particularly important to emphasize the role of feedback in tracking progress over time, as illustrated by the thermometer metaphor, and its function as a conversational tool, exemplified by the therapist's invitation to jointly reflect on the completed questionnaires. When relevant, therapists should also be transparent about any additional uses of the data, such as for supervision or research purposes, and collect consent accordingly.

Lack of progress

All therapists encounter situations in which clients do not progress as expected in therapy. Such situations can be challenging to manage, as they may lead to demotivation and increase the risk of dropout. From an Integrative Systemic Therapy (IST) perspective, a lack of progression is hypothesized to reflect the presence of one or more constraints within the therapeutic process or the client system. In the following vignette, we demonstrate how a therapist may use systematic feedback to identify and address such a constraint.

The client system consists of Lucas (11), his sister Tina (17), and their parents, Tom and May Helen. The family is attending therapy after Lucas reported to a school social worker that he suspects his father of drinking alcohol during weekdays. The vignette takes place at the beginning of the third session, where the therapist has invited all family members to complete age-appropriate PCOMS questionnaires.

Therapist: Okay, everyone, let's take a look at the questionnaires. Would it be okay if we lay them all out on the table so we can see them together?

(The therapist gains approval from all family members and takes a moment to scan their responses.)

So, what catches your attention?

(The therapist intentionally poses an open question to observe who takes the lead and to gain information about family dynamics.)

May Helen: Well . . . it doesn't look like Lucas is feeling okay about how things are going.

Therapist: Mm, yes. That stood out to me as well.

(The therapist looks gently toward Lucas, attuning to his emotional state. Lucas is staring at the table.)

Lucas, would it be okay for you to say a little about this? I notice you marked how things are going in the family closer to the sad face than the smiling face.

Lucas: I don't know . . . nothing really.

(Still looking down, fidgeting with a pencil.)

Therapist: Nothing has been happening since you all started coming here?

(The therapist tentatively tests her working hypothesis about lack of progress, informed by Lucas's feedback.)

Lucas:. . .

Tina: No, it's all the same! Nothing has changed.

Therapist: Okay, so it feels like things are still the same. Tina, help me understand your score on the family line.

(She points to Tina's rating, which is more toward the positive side.)

Tina: I guess I'm not as affected by what's going on at home, since I spend more time out with my friends and stuff.

Therapist: Ah, that makes sense. So, it might be harder for Lucas, since he spends more time at home?

Tina: Mm-hmm.

Therapist: Thanks for explaining that, Tina. Lucas, does that make sense to you as well?

Lucas: Yes.

(He looks up, takes in the room, and then settles his gaze at the therapist.)

(Noticing Lucas's increased engagement, the therapist becomes slightly more directive.)

Therapist: I'm wondering if this connects to what we talked about last time, about you speaking with the school social worker about your dad's drinking?

(Lucas nods.)

Is your dad still drinking at home during the daytime?

(Lucas shakes his head.)

(This disconfirms the therapist's initial hypothesis about ongoing drinking as the primary constraint. Sensing that the constraint may still involve Tom, she shifts her attention.)

Therapist: Okay . . . Dad, help me understand this from your perspective.

Tom: I guess . . . I haven't been drinking during the day since our last session. Hearing the kids talk about it really affected me. I've tried to be more present for them this past week, but it's hard. I don't feel very good.

(Tom appears anxious.)

(The therapist forms a new hypothesis, drawing on the mind and the organization metaframeworks and how they relate to Tom's relationship with the children.)

Therapist: So, the way you're feeling affects how you're able to be with the kids?

Tom: Yes. Since I stopped drinking, my feelings have been harder to deal with. It's uncomfortable. I end up keeping busy with small projects around the house, and I don't really spend time with Lucas as I used to.

Therapist: Is that how it feels to you, Lucas, that your dad is too busy to spend time with you?

(Lucas nods and looks toward his father. Tom now lowers his gaze, shoulders slumping, appearing ashamed.)

Therapist: Okay, this feels important.

(Turning to the whole family.)

Something has changed in your family dynamics. New feelings have come up, and that's created new challenges, but also new opportunities. Let's slow this down together and see how we can use what we're learning here to make things better for all of you.

(The therapist offers Lucas a warm, reassuring smile. Lucas appears relieved, having this difficult but important issue named with support from both the therapist and his family.)

In this vignette involving Lucas and his family, we illustrated how the therapist uses systematic feedback questionnaires by attending closely to the lowest score as a potential indicator of constraint and opportunity for change. The therapist adaptively attunes to both the systematic feedback provided through the questionnaires and the unfolding in-session feedback that emerges through dialogue. This ongoing integration allows her to refine her working hypotheses, identify relevant constraints, and plan the therapeutic process accordingly. Throughout the session, she remains attentive to multiple alliances and actively facilitates collaborative processes between family members.

Had the feedback questionnaires not been used, the therapist would likely not have detected the lack of progress reported by Lucas. As a result, the session might have followed a very different, and potentially less productive course.

Divergent feedback

Divergent feedback relating to outcomes is a common phenomenon in family therapy and often reflects conflictual interaction patterns, differing perspectives among family members, or emerging constraints within the system. In some cases, such divergence may signal a shift in the presenting problem or the emergence of a new therapeutic focus altogether. Attending carefully to these differences is therefore crucial, as they often provide valuable entry points for facilitating change or adjusting the course of therapy. Importantly, divergent feedback should always be approached with curiosity and empathy. In the following vignette, we continue working with the same family introduced previously.

Therapist: Okay, what stands out to you today when you look at how you've filled out the questionnaires?

(This time, no one responds to the invitation.)

Therapist: All right, I'm happy to see that Lucas's score has improved, and I think we should talk more about that. But before we do, I'm also curious about Mum's and Dad's scores. They almost look like mirror images of each other.

(The therapist looks back and forth between Tom and May Helen with a light, surprised expression, carefully signaling curiosity without creating tension. She remains mindful that this appears to relate primarily to the couple subsystem rather than the parent–child subsystem.)

May Helen: Well, ever since Tom stopped drinking, other issues have come up—things that don't really involve the kids.

Tom: Yeah . . . they're important, but . . .

Therapist: Yes, I get it. That makes sense. Some issues have probably been avoided for quite a while, and now that your focus has shifted, they're resurfacing and asking for attention again.

Tom: Yes.

(May Helen looks away, appearing slightly embarrassed.)

Therapist: Since this seems to be a different issue from what initially brought you to therapy, and since it mainly concerns you as a couple, I'd like to suggest that we set up a separate session just for the two of you.

(Having confirmed her working hypothesis that the divergent feedback reflects a new presenting problem in the couple subsystem, the therapist proposes a shift in therapeutic context.)

Tina: Yes, please do. We really don't want to hear about it!

(The family breaks into spontaneous laughter.)

As illustrated in this vignette, divergent feedback may reflect a range of phenomena, from differing perspectives related to the original presenting problem, to constraints within specific subsystems, or even the emergence of a new focus for therapy. Regardless of the underlying reason, attending carefully to divergent scores may open productive conversations about how family members experience situations differently. Such conversations not only help illuminate how problems are maintained but also create opportunities to explore how family members may contribute, both individually and collectively, to meaningful change.

Alliance ruptures and repairs

In couple and family therapy, alliance ruptures often take forms that differ from those typically described in individual therapy. One such pattern is the *split alliance* (Friedlander et al., 2018; Whittaker et al., 2022). Split alliances occur when the therapist develops a stronger alliance with one family member while having a markedly weaker alliance with another. When systematic feedback is used, this may become visible as uneven alliance scores across family members. Such patterns are frequently accompanied by weak alliances between family members themselves and may reflect divergent problem definitions, perceived coalitions, or experiences of being misunderstood or marginalized within the therapeutic process.

Early in therapy, split alliances commonly reflect differences in motivation for attending treatment. Some family members may actively seek help and therefore report a stronger alliance, whereas others may feel pressured to attend and consequently report lower alliance scores (Anderson et al., 2020). This pattern is particularly common when working with adolescents, who are often brought to therapy at the initiative of their parents (Whittaker & Tilden, 2025). Alliance ruptures and persistently low alliance scores are clinically significant, as they are associated with poorer treatment outcomes and an increased risk of dropout if left unaddressed (Friedlander et al., 2018).

Within Integrative Systemic Therapy (IST), alliance ruptures are understood not as failures of therapy, but as important sources of feedback that may signal constraints affecting engagement, collaboration, or emotional safety within the therapeutic process. The meaning of alliance scores, especially low scores, should never be assumed by the therapist but explored collaboratively with the client. While constraints may at times be addressed through explicit constraint questions, this is neither always appropriate nor necessary. In some situations, particularly early in therapy or when the alliance is fragile, constraints are more effectively addressed through relational and dialogical interventions that prioritize engagement, agency, and emotional safety.

In the following vignette, the therapist treats a low alliance score as an indicator of a potential constraint related to motivation and perceived coercion. Rather than posing a direct constraint question, the therapist addresses the rupture by bringing the feedback into the open with curiosity and empathy, inviting the client to elaborate on what the low score might represent. We return once more to the family introduced earlier, joining them at the end of their first session, shortly after they have completed age-appropriate session rating scales. The excerpt captures an exchange between the therapist and the family's teenage daughter, Tina.

Therapist: I hope it's okay to ask you about your alliance score.
(She gestures gently toward Tina's questionnaire.)
I notice that your score is quite a bit lower than the rest of your family's.
(Tina looks at the therapist with apparent disinterest. Drawing on experience with adolescents, the therapist tentatively hypothesizes that Tina's low alliance may reflect feeling pressured to attend.)

Therapist: I wonder if part of this might be that you don't really want to be here, and that this is why your score looks different from the others'.

Tina: It's my stupid little brother's fault that I have to be here. If he hadn't complained about Dad's drinking, I'd be at school right now. I have classes that actually matter!
(She huffs in irritation.)
I don't get why I have to come along.

Therapist: You're absolutely right to ask that question. And it makes a lot of sense that you wouldn't want to be here if it doesn't feel like your problem. At the same time, I think everyone here, including me, is really glad that you did come. How about we make a deal? You don't have to commit to anything long-term. You can just decide one session at a time whether you want to come. I really believe your perspective could be important for all of us.
(Turning briefly to the rest of the family.)
Wouldn't you like Tina to keep coming?
(The others nod.)
(Returning to Tina.)
How does that sound?

Tina: Okay. I'll come next time and see. I do have some opinions I'd like to share.

Therapist: Great. Then it's a deal.

In this vignette, Tina's low alliance score functioned as an early signal of a potential constraint related to her motivation and perceived parental coercion. Rather than attempting to define or resolve the constraint through direct questioning, the therapist prioritized alliance repair by validating Tina's experience and restoring a sense of agency and choice. Framing participation on a session-by-session basis allowed Tina to remain engaged without positioning attendance as an obligation or nonattendance as a failure.

This example illustrates an important distinction in IST between identifying a constraint and addressing it. While constraint questions are often useful for clarifying what maintains a problem sequence, alliance-related constraints may require relational interventions that focus first on engagement, safety, and collaboration. In such cases, repairing the alliance becomes a prerequisite for further therapeutic work rather than something that follows it.

More broadly, the vignette highlights the close relationship between alliance and motivation in couple and family therapy. Therapists must remain attentive to both and be prepared to negotiate participation with clients who feel pressured to attend. This may involve adolescents who would rather be with peers, as well as adults who experience shame, ambivalence, or reluctance to involve a third party. Working effectively with alliance ruptures requires therapists to remain emotionally regulated. It also requires them to validate and normalize client reactions and to collaboratively adjust the therapeutic process to accommodate individual needs without compromising the work with the broader family system.

Concluding remarks

From an Integrative Systemic Therapy (IST) perspective, the use of systematic feedback, as demonstrated throughout this chapter, represents some of the clearest examples of empirically informed and failure-driven learning in clinical practice. This is evident in situations involving lack of therapeutic progress, divergent feedback scores, and alliance ruptures, to name just a few of the clinical challenges illustrated here. Regardless of what the feedback reveals, IST does not view such moments as setbacks. Instead, they are understood as valuable opportunities to adapt therapy in ways that improve outcomes. Feedback functions as the fuel that guides clinical decision-making in real time. When attended to with curiosity and humility, situations that signal challenges to the therapeutic process become opportunities to restore collaboration, refine working hypotheses, and realign therapy with the lived experience of clients.

Taken together, the contents of this chapter illustrate how feedback, whether quantitative, qualitative, or creative, functions in IST as more than a monitoring device; it is a conversational tool for facilitating change. Feedback operates as an ongoing dialogical process that links assessment, alliance building and maintenance, and intervention. Sensitivity to feedback, whether systematic or informal, helps therapists remain problem-focused while also responsive to both progress and constraint. In this way, sustained attention to feedback supports the core aims of IST: promoting collaboration, facilitating adaptive change, and ensuring that therapy remains grounded in the needs and perspectives of the client system.

Self-reflection task

1. To what extent do you currently make use of systematic feedback in your clinical practice?
2. In what ways might the systematic use of feedback enhance your clinical decision-making, collaboration with clients, or therapeutic outcomes?
3. Are there clinical situations or contexts in which the use of systematic feedback may be less appropriate or even counterproductive?

References

Anderson, S. R., Banford Witting, A., Tambling, R. R., Ketring, S. A., & Johnson, L. N. (2020). Pressure to attend therapy, dyadic adjustment, and adverse childhood experiences: Direct and Indirect effects on the therapeutic alliance in couples therapy. *Journal of Marital and Family Therapy*, *46*(2), 366–380. https://doi.org/10.1111/jmft.12394

Anderson, S. R., Johnson, L. N., Miller, R. B., & Barkham, C. C. (2021). The couple relationship scale: A brief measure to facilitate routine outcome monitoring in couple therapy. *Journal of Marital and Family Therapy*, *48*(2), 464–483. https://doi.org/10.1111/jmft.12541

Anderson, S. R., Johnson, L. N., Witting, A. B., Miller, R. B., Bradford, A. B., Hunt, Q. A., & Bean, R. A. (2024). Validation of the intersession alliance measure: Individual, couple, and family versions. *Journal of Marital and Family Therapy*, *50*(3), 589–610. https://doi.org/10.1111/jmft.12702

Anker, M. G., Duncan, B. L., & Sparks, J. A. (2009). Using client feedback to improve couple therapy outcomes: A randomized clinical trial in a naturalistic setting. *Journal of Consulting and Clinical Psychology*, *77*(4), 693–704. https://doi.org/10.1037/a0016062

Barkham, M., De Jong, K., Delgadillo, J., & Lutz, W. (2023). Routine outcome monitoring (ROM) and feedback: Research review and recommendations. *Psychotherapy Research*, *33*(7), 841–855. https://doi.org/10.1080/10503307.2023.2181114

Bergman, H., Kornør, H., Nikolakopoulou, A., Hanssen-Bauer, K., Soares-Weiser, K., Tollefsen, T. K., & Bjørndal, A. (2018). Client feedback in psychological therapy for children and adolescents with mental health problems. *Cochrane Database of Systematic Reviews, 2018*(8). https://doi.org/10.1002/14651858.cd011729.pub2

Chiauzzi, E. (2021). Lessons learned in measurement-based care with youth mental health clients. *Practice Innovations*, *6*(1), 30–41. https://doi.org/10.1037/pri0000129

Cooper, M., Duncan, B., Golden, S., & Toth, K. (2019). Systematic client feedback in therapy for children with psychological difficulties: Pilot cluster randomised controlled trial. *Counselling Psychology Quarterly*, *34*(1), 21–36. https://doi.org/10.1080/09515070.2019.1647142

Cooper, M., Stewart, D., Sparks, J., & Bunting, L. (2013). School-based counseling using systematic feedback: A cohort study evaluating outcomes and predictors of change. *Psychotherapy Research*, *23*(4), 474–488. https://doi.org/10.1080/10503307.2012.735777

Duncan, B. L., Miller, S. D., Sparks, J. A., Claud, D. A., Reynolds, L. R., Brown, J., & Johnson, L. D. (2003a). The session rating scale: Preliminary psychometric properties of a "working" alliance measure. *Journal of Brief Therapy*, *3*(1), 3–12.

Duncan, B. L., Miller, S. D., Sparks, J. A., & Johnson, L. D. (2003b). *Child session rating scale*. Author.

Duncan, B. L., Sparks, J., Miller, S., Bohanske, R., & Claud, D. (2006). Giving youth a voice: A preliminary study of the reliability and validity of a brief outcome measure for children, adolescents, and caretakers. *Journal of Brief Therapy*, *5*, 71–87.

Friedlander, M. L., Escudero, V., Welmers-van de Poll, M. J., & Heatherington, L. (2018). Meta-analysis of the alliance–outcome relation in couple and family therapy. *Psychotherapy*, *55*(4), 356–371. https://doi.org/10.1037/pst0000161

Hannan, C., Lambert, M. J., Harmon, C., Nielsen, S. L., Smart, D. W., Shimokawa, K., & Sutton, S. W. (2004). A lab test and algorithms for identifying clients at risk for treatment failure. *Journal of Clinical Psychology*, *61*(2), 155–163. https://doi.org/10.1002/jclp.20108

Johnson, L. N., Anderson, S. R., & Wagner, K. N. (2025). The marriage and family therapy practice research network: Current findings and a call for collaboration. *European Journal of Mental Health, 20*, 1–9. https://doi.org/10.5708/ejmh.20.2025.0036

Johnson, L. N., Miller, R. B., Bradford, A. B., & Anderson, S. R. (2017). The marriage and family therapy practice research network: Creating a more perfect union between practice and research. *Journal of Marital and Family Therapy*, *43*(4), 561–572. https://doi.org/10.1111/jmft.12238

Lambert, M. J., Whipple, J. L., Hawkins, E. J., Vermeersch, D. A., Nielsen, S. L., & Smart, D. W. (2003). Is it time for clinicians to routinely track patient outcome? A meta-analysis. *Clinical Psychology: Science and Practice*, *10*(3), 288–301. https://doi.org/10.1093/clipsy.bpg025

McLeod, J. (2017). Qualitative methods for routine outcome measurement. In B. E. Wampold & T. Rousmaniere (Eds.), *The cycle of excellence: Using deliberate practice to improve supervision and training* (pp. 97–122). Oxford University Press.

Miller, S. D., Duncan, B. L., Brown, J., Sparks, J. A., & Claud, D. A. (2003). The outcome rating scale: A preliminary study of the reliability, validity, and feasibility of a brief visual analog measure. *Journal of Brief Therapy*, *2*(2), 91–100.

Mindme. (2021). *Hei: The feelings and situations game* [Board game]. Mindme.

Pinsof, W., Zinbarg, R., He, Y., Goldsmith, J., Latta, T., & Lebow, J. (2024). Does the STIC measurement and feedback system improve multisystemic outcomes in individual, couple and family therapy? A randomized clinical trial. *Psychotherapy Research*, *34*(8), 1078–1091. https://doi.org/10.1080/10503307.2023.2283523

Pinsof, W. M., Breunlin, D. C., Russell, W. P., Lebow, J. L., Rampage, C., & Chambers, A. L. (2018). *Integrative systemic therapy: Metaframeworks for problem solving with individuals, couples, and families*. American Psychological Association. https://doi.org/10.1037/0000055-000

Pinsof, W. M., Zinbarg, R. E., Shimokawa, K., Latta, T. A., Goldsmith, J. Z., Knobloch-Fedders, L. M., Chambers, A. L., & Lebow, J. L. (2015). Confirming, validating, and norming the factor structure of systemic therapy inventory of change initial and intersession. *Family Process*, *54*(3), 464–484. https://doi.org/10.1111/famp.12159

Rober, P., Van Tricht, K., & Sundet, R. (2020). 'One step up, but not there yet': Using client feedback to optimise the therapeutic alliance in family therapy. *Journal of Family Therapy*, *43*(1), 46–63. https://doi.org/10.1111/1467-6427.12292

Tilden, T., & Wampold, B. E. (Eds.). (2017). *Routine outcome monitoring in couple and family therapy*. Springer International Publishing. https://doi.org/10.1007/978-3-319-50675-3

Tilden, T., & Whittaker, K. J. (2022). Using ROM in family therapy. *Journal of Clinical Psychology*, *78*(10), 1973–1985. https://doi.org/10.1002/jclp.23398

Whiting, J. B., Fife, S. T., Davis, S. D., Ogles, B. M., & Bailey, R. J. (2025). Corrective experiencing as a common factor in couple therapy: Creating new and positive emotions in relationships. *Family Process*, *64*(4). https://doi.org/10.1111/famp.70087

Whittaker, K. J., Stänicke, E., Johnson, S. U., Solbakken, O. A., & Tilden, T. (2022). Troubled relationships: A retrospective study of how couples with histories of trauma experience therapy. *Journal of Couple & Relationship Therapy*, *22*(1), 1–23. https://doi.org/10.1080/15332691.2022.2053262

Whittaker, K. J., & Tilden, T. (2025). Fellesfaktorer i par og familieterapi [Common factors in couple and family therapy]. In L. Lorås & O. Ness (Eds.), *Håndbok i familieterapi* [Handbook of family therapy] (pp. 83–97). Fagbokforlaget.

Chapter 13

Evaluating and Concluding Therapy

Introduction

Ending therapy often evokes mixed emotions. Families may feel pride in what they have achieved while also experiencing uncertainty about managing independently. Such ambivalence reflects the complexity of relational change. In Integrative Systemic Therapy (IST), the therapist acknowledges and explores these responses while ensuring that the ending supports the family's emerging autonomy. As new interactional patterns are internalized, attention shifts toward generalizing them across contexts, strengthening the family's capacity for self-regulation and adaptation.

Research within systemic and feedback-informed frameworks suggests that endings can be as transformative as beginnings. When conducted with structure and transparency, they consolidate learning, strengthen mastery, and reduce the likelihood of relapse (Husby, 2025; Pinsof et al., 2018). In contrast, unclear or prolonged endings may undermine progress and foster unnecessary dependency. Within IST, termination is understood as part of the systemic loop, offering closure while simultaneously inviting reflection, feedback, and renewed meaning-making.

In this chapter, the Nguyen family serves as a case illustration. Linh and Quang, who immigrated from Vietnam to Fargo, North Dakota in their youth, are raising their two children, Minh (15) and Bao (11). Although the family is generally well adjusted to life in the United States, the parents continue to experience challenges in raising their children within a cultural context different from the one in which they themselves grew up. These differences are related to academic expectations and the use of leisure time, and have contributed to intergenerational tensions.

As therapy approached its conclusion, not only had the core family been involved, but a grandparent and one of the children's closest aunts had also taken part in several sessions. Progress was evident in more open communication and greater mutual understanding. At the same time, the prospect of ending therapy evoked concern about sustaining stability without professional support.

DOI: 10.4324/9781003645337-15

Hearing clients' voices

By the closing phase of therapy, the family's identified concerns have been addressed. Family members have examined problem sequences, attempted solution sequences, and have identified and mitigated the factors that had constrained change. They have acknowledged how the presenting problem(s) had influenced their interactions and they have identified ways to limit its future impact. Initial and, in some cases, later-established goals for therapy have provided a standard for evaluating progress. In particular, the question regarding what would signal that concerns are less troubling now functions as a shared reference point for assessing readiness for concluding therapy.

At this stage, it is important to explore whether the family members feel their progress has been sufficient (Pote et al., 2000). If so, this indicates that the concerns no longer require professional involvement. From a systemic perspective, such a shift is reflected in changed interactional patterns. When these patterns become more flexible and sustainable, change is integrated into everyday relational life.

As therapy moves toward conclusion, the focus shifts from whether progress has occurred to whether the family can sustain change without external support (Husby, 2025). In Integrative Systemic Therapy (IST), termination is understood as part of the ongoing systemic process rather than as a discrete endpoint. Endings unfold through structured conversations in which experiences, hopes, and uncertainties are acknowledged. Such conversations make visible how autonomy and belonging are balanced as the system prepares for continued self-regulation. Questions that invite both confidence and ambivalence can facilitate this transition. For example,

> When you think about the changes you've been trying out with your family, what feels better now, and what still feels somewhat difficult?

Such inquiries normalize ambivalence and clarify how each person's experience of change contributes to the family's collective capacity for adaptation. In this phase, systematic feedback from the family provides a structured framework for mapping both the consolidation of new interactional patterns and areas where change remains fragile within relationships (Tilden & Whittaker, 2022). Endings gain meaning when family members articulate what they are carrying forward and what they are concerned about losing (Lorås, 2021).

The Nguyen family illustrated this process clearly. As therapy moved toward conclusion, Linh expressed pride in increased openness and reduced intergenerational tension, while also voicing concern about sustaining balance under external pressures. Quang described more harmonious routines, yet questioned whether consistency could be maintained without professional guidance. Their reflections suggested a system consolidating new interactional patterns while remaining attentive to potential difficulties in sustaining these changes. Ensuring Bao's voice was included became central. Previously withdrawn during conflicts about academic expectations and cultural transitions, he described relief that arguments had decreased, indicating a shift in the interactional sequence that had organized the concern. At the same time, he acknowledged lingering fear of disappointing his parents. His contribution highlighted both the changes that had taken place in the family and the challenges that remained. Minh expressed excitement about increased independence alongside concern about losing the calm that had developed. His ambivalence reflected how closely his sense of security remained linked to parental cooperation. Bringing these differentiated perspectives into conversation enabled the family to approach emerging tension as recalibration rather than relapse.

As the family demonstrated greater flexibility in holding difference without escalation, the therapist's role shifted accordingly. Introducing termination communicated trust in the family's evolving competence and sustained hope in their continued capacity for adaptation. Within IST, termination becomes a recursive moment in which systemic autonomy is consolidated and confidence in managing future challenges is strengthened.

Although therapy is ideally concluded with mutual agreement between the therapist and the client system, this is not always the case. If the client family is not satisfied or has not reached its stated treatment goals, three options may be considered:

1. Return to exploring the interactional patterns and constraints that characterized the middle phase of therapy.
2. Examine whether the dissatisfaction reflects concern about managing without therapeutic support.
3. Consider referral to another therapist if this may facilitate further progress (Pote et al., 2000).

Generalizing solutions

An essential task in Integrative Systemic Therapy (IST) during the ending phase is to support families in sustaining solution sequences beyond the therapy room (Lorås, 2021; Husby, 2025). A strategy is robust only if it remains functional across contexts. Change is therefore evaluated not by its stability under structured conditions, but by the family's ability to apply it flexibly when similar challenges arise in everyday life. Reflection during this phase helps ensure that emerging interactional patterns are resilient rather than context-dependent. As Meadows (2008) emphasizes, adaptive systems rely on both redundancies, the availability of multiple coordinated strategies, and adaptiveness, the capacity to adjust under changing conditions. Families likewise benefit from having several relational options available rather than relying on a single preferred pattern.

In the Nguyen family, much of the work had centered on reducing tension related to school expectations and daily routines. As the end of therapy approached, the therapist invited reflection on how these collaborative practices might be transferred to other areas of family life. Questions such as, "In what other situations might these strategies be useful?" and "How could you adapt what you have learned here to similar challenges?" supported this exploration. Linh suggested that weekly check-ins could also assist with planning family gatherings or organizing household responsibilities. Quang noted that brief coordination discussions might prevent misunderstandings when managing finances. Through these conversations, the family began to understand their strategies not as isolated techniques, but as transferable relational practices. This shift strengthened systemic flexibility (Russell et al., 2023).

To consolidate this learning, the therapist invited each family member to identify situations outside therapy in which the newly developed practices might be applied. This conversation was not intended as a checklist exercise, but as a way of strengthening ownership of the change process. Bao recognized that the communication strategies supporting him with schoolwork could also help when navigating peer pressure. Linh and Quang noted that the calm coordination they had practiced during earlier conflicts could be useful during stressful mornings or joint decision-making. The therapist further asked, "What might make it harder to use these strategies in those moments?" and "What could help you remember the strategies when stress increases?" Such questions draw attention to potential constraints and encourage anticipation rather than reaction. This anticipatory stance strengthens the durability of change within a systemic framework. By explicitly linking therapeutic learning to everyday contexts, the family began to understand progress as embedded in ongoing interaction rather than dependent on the therapist's presence. Linh and Quang increasingly used repair strategies in minor tensions, such as disagreements about chores or social plans. For Bao and Minh, this consistency fostered predictability and relational safety. In IST, such shifts mark the movement from externally supported regulation to internally coordinated self-regulation within the family system (Pinsof et al., 2018; Lorås, 2021).

A final step in the generalization process involved inviting the family to name the specific practices they wished to carry forward. Each member articulated what had changed and which tools felt most reliable. Linh highlighted her capacity to pause before reacting. Quang emphasized remaining engaged rather than withdrawing. Bao described increased confidence in expressing his views, and Minh noted feeling calmer when disagreements were handled with composure. Making these practices explicit reinforced that sustaining change is a shared responsibility. The therapist then asked, "If you were to choose the tools that have been most helpful for you as a family to carry forward, which would they be?" This concluding conversation clarified the family's sense of competence and created a natural transition to the next phase of work: preparing for how these practices could be maintained under renewed pressure (Husby, 2025).

Preventing relapse

In Integrative Systemic Therapy (IST), relapse is not framed as failure but as part of long-term adaptation. Setbacks are understood as signals of strain within the system rather than evidence that the work has been ineffective (Whittaker & Lorås, 2025). This perspective reduces shame and reinforces the family's confidence in responding collaboratively to renewed pressure. Thus, an initial step is to normalize that familiar stressors or new demands may reappear (Lorås, 2021). Under strain, systems tend to revert to established interactional patterns, even when these patterns are unhelpful. Anticipating such shifts increases the likelihood that emerging cycles can be interrupted before escalating. Meadows (2008) emphasizes that adaptive systems detect pressure early and adjust accordingly. In therapy, this translates into identifying likely triggers, early signals, and coordinated responses in advance.

The Nguyen family illustrated this process. Although Bao's academic functioning had improved, Linh and Quang anticipated that transitions, such as a new school year or changes in work schedules, could destabilize recent gains. By applying constraint theory (Breunlin, 1999) in structured "what if" conversations, the therapist helped the family reflect on how they wished to respond if tension increased. One early signal was Bao withdrawing when overwhelmed by expectations. By redefining withdrawal as a cue for parental coordination rather than as a problem to correct, Linh and Quang were better positioned to intervene early and prevent escalation. Relapse prevention is most effective when framed as preparation for continued growth rather than as protection against failure. The aim is not to eliminate future difficulty, but to strengthen the family's capacity to recognize strain, coordinate responses, and adjust collaboratively.

To support this work, the therapist and family may co-construct a brief relapse map consisting of four elements:

1. Likely triggers, such as schedule changes or illness
2. Early signs for each member
3. Immediate stabilizers
4. Agreed follow-up steps.

In the Nguyen family, the map included transitions in school or work schedules as triggers, Bao's withdrawal, Linh's increased directiveness, and Quang's tendency to disengage as early signals. Stabilizing responses were summarized in three shared principles: "pause before reacting," "use repair signals," and "keep routines visible." The children contributed actively. Bao committed to expressing when he felt pressured, and Minh requested that weekly check-ins continue. Writing these agreements down transformed intentions into shared commitments, a process Husby (2025) identifies as central to sustaining change beyond therapy. The map was placed visibly in the kitchen, functioning as a shared reference point when tension increased. Its purpose was coordination rather than control.

Systematic feedback may remain useful after concluding therapy as a monitoring structure; strengthening support beyond the immediate family further expands adaptive capacity. Identifying trusted individuals or external resources increases resilience by linking internal coordination with broader relational networks. Linh named a close friend she could contact when overwhelmed, and Quang mentioned a colleague. The sessions, which included the grandparent and the aunt, were especially successful, leading to increased understanding among participating family members and to more practical support in daily life. Bao was particularly delighted with the outcome, as the sessions contributed to an even closer relationship with his aunt. They developed a shared enjoyment of weekend outings together. These weekends also gave Linh and Quang opportunities to spend time with Minh on his terms, without needing to respond to Bao's needs. Integrating such support reduces isolation and reinforces the family's ability to respond flexibly under strain.

A brief weekly check-in during the first month can help consolidate emerging routines. Each member may rate how well current practices are functioning and identify one minor adjustment. If ratings decline, the family revisits the relapse map and adapts accordingly. In some cases, a brief follow-up session may be arranged to review feedback using structured tools described in Chapter 12 (Russell et al., 2023).

Some families also benefit from agreeing on a transparent reentry protocol before therapy concludes. Together, the therapist and client family may define what developments would warrant renewed contact, such as sustained escalation or persistent school avoidance, and clarify how such contact would be initiated. Within IST, this does not undermine autonomy. Rather, it establishes a clear pathway for support should new constraints emerge. In this way, relapse prevention becomes integrated into the logic of concluding therapy itself. Closure reinforces autonomy and resilience while maintaining clarity about how support can be accessed if needed. Families leave therapy not with an expectation of stability, but with confidence in their collective capacity to adapt under changing conditions.

Evaluating the process

Evaluation is a central part of ending therapy. As therapy approaches conclusion, family members are invited to reflect on what the process has meant for them and how change has unfolded (Stratton et al., 2009). Within Integrative Systemic Therapy (IST), evaluation is not conceptualized as an external measure of outcome, but as a continuation of the collaborative conversations that have shaped the work from the outset. It provides space to recognize what has supported change, what has remained challenging, and how the therapeutic relationship has contributed to shifts within the system.

As described in Chapter 12, systematic feedback offers a structured yet flexible framework for facilitating such reflection. Revisiting feedback in the final phase allows families to consider developments in relational patterns, alliance, and overall functioning across system levels. Rather than introducing a new evaluative procedure, this step extends the feedback-informed stance already embedded in the therapy process. Evaluation thus becomes a natural continuation of shared inquiry rather than a separate closing exercise. Systematic feedback in IST is not limited to formal instruments. It may also be elicited through ongoing therapeutic conversations or developmentally adapted methods that invite participation across ages. The therapist might ask:

- "What aspects of our conversations have been most helpful?"
- "What felt less helpful?"
- "What contributed to a constructive conversation between us?"
- "What may have limited our collaboration?"
- "Is there anything you wish we had done differently?"

Such questions underscore that evaluation concerns shared meaning-making rather than judgment of success or failure. Because many clients find it difficult to offer critical feedback, particularly near the end of therapy, evaluation should feel like a continuation of a relational process in which their perspectives have consistently been valued. In line with the child-focused stance of IST, feedback may also be expressed through drawings, brief narratives, scaled questions, or symbolic representations adapted to the child's developmental level and interests. These forms broaden participation and reduce the risk that evaluation gives privilege to adult narratives.

The therapist may further frame feedback as a shared learning opportunity. For example, "If I were to meet another family facing similar challenges, what advice would you give me about how to be most helpful?" Questions of this kind invite reflexivity and often open space for thoughtful and candid reflection. Within IST, such use of systematic feedback honors clients' expertise, reinforces their sense of agency, and consolidates the collaborative foundation of systemic change. Evaluation thus strengthens the family's awareness of how their own contributions have shaped both process and outcome.

Concluding remarks

The ending phase is an integral component of the therapeutic process. Within Integrative Systemic Therapy (IST), concluding therapy represents a transitional moment in which progress is consolidated, relational capacities are strengthened, and readiness for future adaptation is affirmed. Attending carefully to each voice is particularly important at this stage. While parents may describe change in terms of reduced conflict or improved routines, children and adolescents may experience the process differently. Actively inviting their perspectives ensures that evaluation reflects lived experience across the system rather than adult-defined narratives.

In practice, closure requires intention and structure. Explicit conversations about concluding therapy reduce dependency, reinforce autonomy, and clarify the family's capacity to adapt collectively. Preparing for potential setbacks strengthens this autonomy when framed as anticipation rather than protection. Importantly, such preparation must include how children understand and interpret future challenges, not only how adults conceptualize them.

Within IST, endings reflect the overall logic of the approach. Therapy is collaborative, feedback-informed, and grounded in the understanding that constraints may reappear in new forms over time. By maintaining focus on relational practices, planning frameworks, and systematic feedback, therapists support families in sustaining change independently. Ensuring developmentally appropriate participation strengthens children's roles as active contributors within the system.

Evaluation remains central in this final phase. When therapists invite reflection, whether through conversation or systematic feedback, each member's perspective is acknowledged as meaningful. Without intentional inclusion, evaluation risks privileging adult voices and overlooking how change has been experienced by younger members. When all perspectives are integrated, closure becomes reflective and empowering rather than procedural.

Ultimately, the aim of ending therapy is not to eliminate future difficulty but to enhance the family's collective competence in responding to it. Closure thus becomes an active and systemic process, distributing agency across members and reinforcing confidence in their adaptive capacity beyond the therapy context.

Self-reflection task

1. How do you determine, in collaboration with the family, that it is the right time to end therapy?
2. How can you help families prepare for setbacks in ways that strengthen autonomy rather than create dependency?
3. In what ways can evaluation and feedback during the ending phase deepen the family's sense of ownership and competence?

References

Breunlin, D. C. (1999). Toward a theory of constraints. *Journal of Marital and Family Therapy*, *25*(3), 365–382. https://doi.org/10.1111/j.1752-0606.1999.tb00254.x

Husby, V. (2025). *Ferdighetstrening i faglig avslutning av behandlingsforløp* [Skills training in professional termination of treatment]. Fagbokforlaget.

Lorås, L. (2021). Faser i relasjonelle samtaler [Phases in relational conversations]. In L. Lorås & J. C. V. Christiansen (Eds.), *Samtaler i relasjonelt arbeid* [Conversations in relational work] (pp. 67–80). Fagbokforlaget.

Meadows, D. (2008). *Thinking in systems: A primer*. Chelsea Green Publishing.

Pinsof, W. M., Breunlin, D. C., Russell, W. P., Lebow, J. L., Rampage, C., & Chambers, A. L. (2018). *Integrative systemic therapy. Metaframeworks for problem solving with individuals, couples and families*. American Psychological Association. https://doi.org/10.1037/0000055-000

Pote, H., Stratton, P., Cottrell, D., Bostion, P., Shapiro, D., & Hanks, H. (2000). *The Leeds systemic family therapy manual*. Leeds Family Therapy Research Center.

Russell, W. P., Breunlin, D. C., & Lofton, H. C. (2023). Integrative systemic therapy: A feedback-driven perspective. *Fokus på Familien* [Focus on the family], *4*(51), 293–314. https://doi.org/10.18261/fokus.51.4.3

Stratton, P., Pote, H., Cottrell, D., Boston, P., Shapiro, D., & Hanks, H. (2009). *The Leeds systemic family therapy manual: Therapist adherence protocol, training edition*. Leeds, LFTRC.

Tilden, T., & Whittaker, K. J. (2022). Using ROM in family therapy. *Journal of Clinical Psychology*, *78*(10), 1973–1985. https://doi.org/10.1002/jclp.23398

Whittaker, K. J., & Lorås, L. (2025). Integrativ systemisk terapi [Integrative systemic therapy]. In L. Lorås & O. Ness (Eds.), *Håndbok i familieterapi* [Handbook in family therapy] (pp. 283–298). Fagbokforlaget.

Chapter 14
Concluding Comments

This book presents Integrative Systemic Therapy (IST) as a comprehensive and evolving framework for working with children, adolescents, and their families. Each chapter has contributed a vital part of this framework, from its historical and theoretical foundations to its clinical application across the phases of therapy and the specific challenges and opportunities that arise when working with young people in their family systems. The purpose of this final chapter is not to restate what has already been written, but to put the book in perspective, consider why IST matters, and highlight how the framework prepares therapists for the future of systemic practice.

A field in need of renewal

Family therapy emerged from the conviction that human difficulties must be understood relationally rather than as individual defects (Jensen & Ulleberg, 2019). General systems theory (GST) introduced a revolutionary shift from linear causality to circular processes and interactional patterns (von Bertalanffy, 1969). However, while GST provided a powerful meta-language, it did not in itself offer sufficiently precise conceptual tools for guiding clinical decision-making in work with families. The systemic tradition often remained abstract, making translation into moment-to-moment therapeutic practice challenging (Lorås, 2017).

In systemic family therapy more broadly, theory in some contexts appears to have lost its central position. As Lebow (2025) notes, increasing emphasis on techniques, manuals, and common factors has sometimes led to a diminished focus on coherent theoretical frameworks. When theory recedes into the background, clinical work risks becoming fragmented, guided more by immediate pragmatism than by an integrated understanding of change processes. The challenge for systemic practice is therefore not only to preserve its theoretical heritage but to articulate it in ways that remain conceptually rigorous and clinically actionable.

DOI: 10.4324/9781003645337-16

Family systems theory developed in response to this need by operationalizing systemic principles within observable interactional processes and empirically supported models of family functioning (Priest & Lorås, 2026). It moved systemic thinking from metaphor to structured intervention, providing clinically applicable concepts for understanding regulation, hierarchy, boundaries, and developmental transitions in families.

Building on this foundation, Integrative Systemic Therapy (IST) conceptualizes families as autonomous and adaptive systems (He et al., 2023). Autonomy refers to the system's capacity to sustain its identity and coherence, while adaptation refers to its ability to reorganize in response to developmental and contextual demands (Priest, 2025). When autonomy dominates without sufficient adaptation, rigidity emerges; when adaptation occurs without stable autonomy, coherence weakens. Family resilience depends on maintaining both processes simultaneously. Efforts to maintain this balance occur within a complex, multilevel system shaped by factors that both support and constrain it. In IST, these factors are described through the hypothesizing metaframeworks—organization, culture, gender, development, mind, biology, and spirituality.

Clinical difficulties arise when the balance of autonomy and adaptation breaks down. A child's refusal to attend school, for example, may express not only individual anxiety but also systemic imbalances in parental coordination, expectations, and the family's ability to reorganize routines. An adolescent's withdrawal from family life may signal a developmental struggle between emerging individuality and the need for rigid social belonging. Parents engaged in ongoing conflict may activate persistent threat, creating constraints that limit the system's adaptive capacity. In each situation, the therapeutic task is not to correct one person's behavior but to help the family recalibrate autonomy and adaptation so that identity and growth can coexist.

The perspective offered by IST is both theoretical and practical in nature. It provides a scientifically grounded language for describing where families become constrained and a reliable compass for guiding systemic change (Whittaker & Lorås, 2023). When therapy is grounded in the interplay between autonomy and adaptation, interventions extend beyond surface behaviors and address presenting concerns by targeting the underlying organizational processes that sustain family functioning over time and across various contexts.

IST advances family systems theory by translating these principles into operational tools such as problem sequences, solution sequences, constraints, feedback, and recursive planning (Pinsof et al., 2018). These concepts are functional rather than merely descriptive. They can be observed, mapped, and reorganized in real time. In doing so, IST provides a structured decision architecture that integrates theory, empirical grounding, and clinical responsiveness.

Working with families in practice

In Integrative Systemic Therapy (IST), families are understood as autonomous and adaptive systems in which each member's behavior both shapes and is shaped by ongoing interaction (Lorås & Whittaker, 2026). Families who seek therapy present a broad spectrum of difficulties. Some arrive in acute crisis because a child refuses to attend school. Others come because an adolescent feels overwhelmed by anxiety, isolation, or pressure to perform. Parents may struggle with questions about discipline, managing digital life, or supporting a child facing developmental challenges. Still others seek help when marital conflict affects parenting, or when rivalry between siblings destabilizes the household. What unites these situations is that problems rarely exist in isolation. They develop as sequences of interaction in which every action becomes both a response to and a trigger for others. A teenager's withdrawal may heighten parental worry, which in turn fuels controlling behavior and increases the adolescent's distance. A parent's criticism may evoke defensiveness in the other parent, escalating conflict and reducing coordination. Over time, such patterns reinforce themselves, making relational difficulties appear as individual symptoms rather than systemic ones.

IST provides therapists with conceptual and practical tools to map interactional sequences, identify where they are maintained, and support families in developing new patterns that promote connection and flexibility (Pinsof et al., 2018). Change in IST is not expected to follow a straight line. Families often experience periods of progress followed by setbacks when new or hidden constraints interfere with implementation. Constraints can take many forms, including unresolved couple conflict, financial stress, cultural narratives about parenting, or pressures from external systems such as schools, child welfare services, or healthcare providers. Understanding these constraints gives therapists a framework for identifying where change is hindered and for restoring flexibility within the system (Breunlin, 1999).

Thus, the central task for the integrative systemic therapist is not to push against resistance but to view it as valuable information about where the family system struggles to adapt. By addressing constraints, exploring cultural expectations, or coordinating with external networks, the therapist helps the family regain momentum toward sustainable change. This capacity for flexibility defines IST in practice: therapy adjusts to the realities of family life while remaining guided by a coherent theoretical and decision-making framework (Russell et al., 2022).

Children and adolescents as contributors

In Integrative Systemic Therapy (IST), the principle of multivoicedness is a central tenet. Every member of the family system contributes to its patterns of interaction, and therapy becomes most effective when all these voices are heard and acknowledged. The inclusion of children and adolescents in therapy, therefore, represents a natural extension of the systemic foundation of IST. In this sense, multivoicedness is not merely an ethical stance but a regulatory principle: the system's adaptive capacity depends on the inclusion of diverse perspectives across generations.

A distinctive contribution of IST is its commitment to involving children and adolescents as active participants in the therapeutic process. Young people are often positioned as passive recipients of adult agendas or as "identified patients" carrying the visible symptoms of family distress (Øvreeide, 2022). IST challenges this assumption by viewing them as essential contributors whose perspectives and agency are crucial for meaningful change. In practice, this means creating developmentally sensitive ways for children to describe their experiences, formulating questions that invite their perspectives, and recognizing that their observations often reveal relational dynamics that adults do not see. A child may express how parental conflict influences their sense of safety, while an adolescent might articulate the tension between a desire for independence and the family's expectations for cohesion. Such contributions deepen the therapist's systemic understanding and frequently reshape the direction of intervention.

The inclusion of children in therapy is grounded in an understanding of their inherent relational capacities. Øvreeide (2022) describes how children are born with a prosocial orientation, a natural tendency to contribute positively to others and to seek mutual connection. When adults respond with genuine curiosity and openness to children's perspectives, the child experiences being "good for someone." This experience nurtures vitality, agency, and trust in relationships. When children's initiatives are ignored or undervalued, this vitality diminishes and defensive or withdrawn patterns may take their place. Within therapy, acknowledging children's potential for contribution has a similar effect: when their voices are heard and valued, they experience themselves as active participants whose presence makes a difference. This strengthens both their sense of autonomy and the family's collective ability to adapt.

Within IST, including children in therapy is not simply a matter of inviting their opinions but of recognizing their innate dialogical capacities. Children seek connection and meaning through dialogue yet depend on adults to help regulate emotions and give language to their experiences (Øvreeide, 2022). When therapists create settings where children, parents, and therapists share attention to a common concern, such as a triangulated dialogue, the child's individuality is affirmed within a context of belonging. This shared focus helps the family develop a more coherent understanding of each member's experience and supports the system's ability to adapt to developmental transitions.

In contemporary contexts, this stance is critical. Children and adolescents grow up in environments shaped by digital communication, cultural diversity, and changing understandings of identity and belonging. Their perspectives cannot be assumed to mirror those of their parents; they bring unique experiences shaped by peer relationships, online cultures, and rapidly evolving developmental expectations. Recognizing their relational competence enables therapists to engage them as co-constructors of systemic change rather than as informants of adult-defined concerns. This perspective aligns with IST's focus on interaction, reciprocity, and adaptation, ensuring that therapy supports the family's capacity for connection, growth, and flexibility (Pinsof et al., 2018).

Therapy as feedback-driven and collaborative

In Integrative Systemic Therapy (IST), therapy is understood as a feedback-driven collaborative process rather than a linear journey from problem to solution (Pinsof et al., 2018). Change unfolds through cycles of observation, reflection, and adjustment, where new experiences and feedback continually refine and reshape understanding. IST reflects the systemic principle that meaning emerges through dialogue between therapist and family rather than through detached analysis (Jensen & Ulleberg, 2019). Each conversation therefore becomes both an exploration of existing patterns and a testing ground for alternative sequences.

This process is structured through the blueprint for therapy, which functions as a decision architecture guiding hypothesizing, planning, conversing, and reading feedback. The blueprint ensures that therapy remains coherent across phases while allowing flexibility in response to new information. The web of human experience complements this structure by widening the therapist's lens, situating difficulties within psychological, biological, cultural, developmental, and organizational contexts (Whittaker & Tilden, 2022; Russell et al., 2022). Together, these frameworks support disciplined curiosity: hypotheses are formed, tested, refined, or reformulated in light of feedback (Tilden, 2023).

At the core of this logic lies the essence diagram, the functional sequence that links problem definition, solution experimentation, identification of constraints, and renewed planning. The hypothesis and planning matrix provides the therapist with structured options for intervention while preserving systemic coherence. Rather than prescribing techniques, they organize decision-making so that interventions remain theoretically anchored and contextually responsive.

Families are not passive recipients of professional expertise but partners in an ongoing process of hypothesis testing and adaptation. Each emotional shift, clarification, or corrective response becomes information within the feedback loop. When therapy slows or appears stuck, IST does not attribute failure to resistance but revisits constraints that may be limiting flexibility (Breunlin, 1999). Such moments are not interruptions of therapy but expressions of the system's protective organization, inviting renewed mapping and recalibration.

In this way, IST embodies disciplined flexibility. Therapy is not a sequence of isolated techniques, but a structured, feedback-driven conversation, guided by the blueprint, informed by the web of human experience, organized through the hypothesis and planning matrix, continually refined through systematic feedback. Across all phases, from mapping problem sequences to consolidating endings, this architecture sustains coherence while honoring complexity. Change becomes a co-created process grounded in theory, structured through tools, and responsive to lived experience.

Endings as beginnings

Within Integrative Systemic Therapy (IST), the final phase of therapy marks a shift from supported change to self-sustained adaptation (Lorås, 2021). Families often meet this phase with mixed emotions: pride in what has been achieved and apprehension about managing without the therapist's presence. Rather than interpreting this ambivalence as resistance, IST views it as a natural reflection of systemic transition (Whittaker & Lorås, 2025).

Endings provide a space for integration and reflection. In the final sessions, families are invited to reflect on their therapeutic journey, recognize the changes that have occurred, and understand how these changes have emerged through their own efforts and collaboration (Lorås, 2021). Through this reflection, families begin to realize that the capacities strengthened in therapy, such as communication, regulation, and flexibility, are not external skills learned from the therapist but resources that already exist within their own system. Recognizing this shifts the experience of therapy from something received to something co-created.

As families begin to discuss how they will meet future challenges, the conversation moves naturally from reflection to preparation. They are not ending a process, but rehearsing continuity. Parents may explore how to sustain cooperation through new developmental stages, while adolescents may reflect on how to maintain independence without losing connection. In this way, the focus of therapy expands from solving specific problems to strengthening the family's ongoing ability to adapt together as a unit. Such conversations transform uncertainty into readiness and reveal a growing confidence in the family's own capacity for renewal and change.

By approaching endings as beginnings, IST reinforces its systemic view of change as feedback-driven and ongoing. Families do not leave therapy with the belief that difficulties will never return but with confidence in their ability to recognize, interpret, and reorganize patterns when challenges arise again (Lorås, 2021). The end of therapy thus becomes a symbolic handover of authorship: the therapist steps back, allowing the family to continue shaping its own development. In this way, closure is not the end of therapy's influence but its most enduring expression, an affirmation that adaptation, dialogue, and resilience remain active within the family system long after the sessions conclude.

Implications for the future of family therapy

The implications of Integrative Systemic Therapy (IST) for the future of family therapy are substantial. IST demonstrates that a systemic approach can be both scientifically grounded and clinically relevant. By integrating testable hypotheses, structured feedback, and systemic analysis, the framework bridges the long-standing divide between theory and practice (Pinsof et al., 2018). IST shows that family therapy can remain faithful to its relational foundations while also being evidence-informed and accountable in contemporary clinical contexts.

Equally important, IST points toward the renewal of systems theory itself. The foundational insights of family systems theory offer a powerful lens for understanding human interaction; however, they must evolve in dialogue with advancements in science and society. Concepts such as autonomy and adaptation provide a precise and dynamic language for describing how families sustain their identity while reorganizing under pressure (Priest, 2025). In doing so, IST connects systemic practice to broader scientific and social understandings of complexity, interdependence, and change.

IST also represents a renewed ethical and professional stance within the field (Whittaker & Lorås, 2023). Its feedback-driven and structured approach ensures that therapists remain learners as well as guides. This approach strengthens accountability without reducing therapy to a technical procedure. It preserves the relational and dialogical core of systemic work while ensuring that practice is transparent, reflexive, and responsive to diversity.

These implications are particularly significant for work with children and adolescents. Young people today grow up within increasingly complex social ecologies shaped by digital environments, shifting cultural identities, academic pressures, and evolving family structures. Such intersecting influences cannot be reduced to individual symptomatology. IST's integration of the blueprint, the web of human experience, and systematic feedback enables therapists to engage this complexity without losing systemic coherence. By combining developmental sensitivity with structured decision-making tools, IST strengthens family therapy's ability to support young people within the relational systems that shape their development.

Moreover, IST provides the field with something that has been missing in recent decades: a unifying and empirically supported metaframework (Lorås & Whittaker, 2026). It brings coherence to systemic practice without constraining it to a single model. By drawing on the best available knowledge across disciplines, IST positions family therapy as both a rigorous and creative enterprise that honors complexity while remaining accessible to practitioners and policymakers alike. As noted by Priest and Lorås (2026), systemic practice must demonstrate its value not only through compelling narratives but through frameworks that link reflection, structure, and evidence in meaningful ways.

Looking ahead, the strength of family therapy will depend on its ability to articulate its relevance within contemporary health and social systems. IST offers precisely that foundation. It provides the field with a shared conceptual language, a coherent set of clinical tools, and a framework that reaffirms what has always been at the heart of systemic practice: that change emerges through relationships, that knowledge is co-created, and that families hold within them the potential for renewal.

Concluding remarks

As this book draws to a close, it is natural to return to the central promise of Integrative Systemic Therapy (IST). IST is not concerned with repairing individual children and adolescents in isolation but with helping families recognize and reorganize the patterns that shape their lives. The therapist's task is to support families in interrupting destructive sequences, strengthening communication, and developing relational processes that sustain balance and resilience. In this work, belonging and individuality are not opposing forces but interdependent dynamics that allow families to remain connected while continuing to grow.

Families who enter therapy often feel caught in recurring difficulties that appear fixed and unchangeable. Through systemic exploration, they begin to recognize that what seems entrenched is sustained through interaction and can therefore be reorganized. As relationships shift, new possibilities emerge. Over time, families leave therapy with a renewed sense of agency, understanding themselves not as isolated individuals carrying burdens alone but as relational systems capable of adaptation and growth. This movement from perceived immobility to experienced flexibility lies at the heart of IST's contribution.

IST itself remains an evolving framework. It is not a closed system, but a living architecture refined through feedback, reflection, and collaboration. Its strength lies in its openness to new knowledge and its ability to integrate insights across disciplines without losing its systemic coherence. What remains constant is its commitment to families as active partners in change, to the dialogue between theory and practice, and to the complexity of human relationships (Russell et al., 2022).

In a world characterized by uncertainty and rapid transformation, the principles of IST retain their relevance. They affirm that resilience grows from connection rather than control, that adaptation is sustained through collaborative engagement, and that within every family there exists the potential for renewal. The therapist's role is not to impose change but to illuminate possibilities, helping families recognize their strengths and trust their ongoing capacity for reorganization. In this sense, therapy does not end with the final session; it continues as part of the family's evolving narrative of meaning, adaptation, and hope.

References

Breunlin, D. C. (1999). Toward a theory of constraints. *Journal of Marital and Family Therapy*, *25*(3), 365–382. https://doi.org/10.1111/j.1752-0606.1999.tb00254.x

He, Y., Hardy, N. R., Fisher, A. R., & Lokotama, I. (2023). Development of the integrative systemic therapist. *Fokus på Familien* [Focus on the family], *4*(51), 315–331. https://doi.org/10.18261/fokus.51.4.4

Jensen, P., & Ulleberg, I. (2019). *Mellom ordene- kommunikasjon i profesjonell praksis* [Between words—Communication in professional practice]. Gyldendal.

Lebow, J. (2025). Reflections about the place of theory in today's couple and family therapy. *Australian and New Zealand Journal of Family Therapy*, *46*(4), e70038. https://doi.org/10.1002/anzf.70038

Lorås, L. (2017). *The map of competences in systemic therapy. A qualitative study of the systemic competences in Norwegian child and adolescent mental health that target the associated abnormal psychosocial situations in axis 5 (ICD-10).* [Doctoral thesis]. East London University in conjunction with the Tavistock Clinic.

Lorås, L. (2021). Faser i relasjonelle samtaler [Phases in relational conversations]. In L. Lorås & J. C. V. Christiansen (Eds.), *Samtaler i relasjonelt arbeid* [Conversations in relational work] (pp. 67–80). Fagbokforlaget.

Lorås, L., & Whittaker, K. J. (2026). Integrative systemic therapy. In O. Smoliak, E. Tseliou, T. Strong, S. Bava, & P. Muntigl (Eds.), *The Routledge international handbook of postmodern therapies* (pp. 249–262). Routledge.

Øvreeide, H. (2022). Barns godhet [Children's goodness]. *Fokus på Familien* [Focus on the family], *4*(50), 274–290. https://doi.org/10.18261/fokus.50.4.2

Pinsof, W. M., Breunlin, D. C., Russell, W. P., Lebow, J. L., Rampage, C., & Chambers, A. L. (2018). *Integrative systemic therapy: Metaframeworks for problem solving with individuals, couples, and families*. American Psychological Association. https://doi.org/10.1037/0000055-000

Priest, J. (2025). *The science of family systems theory*. Routledge.

Priest, J., & Lorås, L. (2026). *Familiesystemteori. Teori, evidens og praksis* [Family systems theory. Theory, evidence and practice]. Fagbokforlaget.

Russell, W. P., Breunlin, D. C., & Sahebi, B. (2022). *Integrative systemic therapy in practice: A clinician's handbook*. Routledge.

Tilden, T. (2023). Hvilken nytte har vi av modell? [What use do we have for models?]. *Fokus på Familien* [Focus on the family], *4*(51), 270–292. https://doi.org/10.18261/fokus.51.4.2

von Bertalanffy, L. (1969). *General system theory: Foundations, development, applications*. George Braziller.

Whittaker, K. J., & Lorås, L. (2023). Integrativ Systemisk Terapi som tilnærming i arbeid med sammensatte problemer [Integrative Systemic Therapy as a therapeutic approach to compounded problems]. *Fokus på familien* [Focus on the family], *4*(51), 332–348. https://doi.org/10.18261/fokus.51.4.5

Whittaker, K. J., & Tilden, T. (2022). Integrativ systemisk terapi: Metateori og psykoterapeutisk praksis [Integrative Systemic Therapy: Metatheory and Psychotherapeutic Practice]. *Fokus på Familien* [Focus on the family], *3*(49), 190–206. https://doi.org/10.18261/fokus.50.3.2

Whittaker, K. J., & Tilden, T. (2025). Fellesfaktorer i par og familieterapi [Common factors in couple and family therapy]. In L. Lorås & O. Ness (Eds.), *Håndbok i familieterapi* [Handbook in family therapy] (pp. 83–97). Fagbokforlaget.

Index

Note: Page numbers in *italics* indicate figures; page numbers in **bold** indicate tables.

For Product Safety Concerns and Information please contact our EU
representative GPSR@taylorandfrancis.com
Taylor & Francis Verlag GmbH, Kaufingerstraße 24, 80331 München, Germany

www.ingramcontent.com/pod-product-compliance
Ingram Content Group UK Ltd.
Pitfield, Milton Keynes, MK11 3LW, UK
UKHW022020211026
476876UK00010B/453

* 9 7 8 1 0 4 1 0 8 4 2 9 7 *